BLACKMAN REDEMPTION

BOOK TWO

THE RISE AND FALL OF JA-MAI-CA

BY

MICHELLE JEAN

Blackman Redemption Book Two The Rise and Fall of Ja-Mai-Ca.

Lord where do I begin

Where do I start because the situation looks grim?

Jamaica

The sinking of Port Royal

Hurricane Gilbert, Ivan and Andrew

You have countless storms

More recently you had a minor earthquake

Let's not forget your debt load of over 18.2 billion U.S.

Your economy is declining

No new investments coming into the country

Your education system lags behind that of developed nations

Aah yes I have a smile on my face but it is not a smile of joy but it is a smile anyway.

My Jamaican people where do I start with you because I did tell you the bell sounds and you are on your last leg if you do not wake up and repent redeem yourself.

Laade God wooo nelly retribution time draws near because none of you know your future and that the angels walk amongst you.

You are living by a thread right now and don't know it because disaster is at your doorstep and none of you know it. Trust me soon Jamaica will be no more. People a lot of are going to die. Unna a go suffa.

Remember ole time people sey God a wait fi all di good people dem fi dead before im unleash his fury on the island. Well di good people dem gaane anna suffaration time now.

Jamaican's from Africa you came

To nowhere you go

Hell bound

Confused

Bound

Enslaved yet again

Jamaica it isn't pretty is it. There is no more wakeup call for the island. Now death cometh like a thief in the night.

Tell me something Jamaica where is your future?

Also truly tell me why is it that when I dream see your Prime Minister I dream him in full black and he is leading you down a precipit. Leading you down the stairs and not up the stairs. Well im gaane now and his loada man as unnu call him gaane now. Now unnu ave a new Prime Minister and if she does not clean up the island and soon woo nelly. It no matta anyway because sey she cannot save you from what is to come because the island is far gone.

Tell me something Jamaica what do you own now well a part from an 18.2 billion dollar US debt that neither you nor your future generation can pay off. Not even the richest Jamaica has this much money.

Tell me how can an island so small rack up such a massive debt?

Right now you currently own nothing.

You don't even own the island you live on. Not even the clothes on your backs.

Let me rack it up for you:

- *Air Jamaica – Air God- GONE.*

  New name, new company, new owners – yes Trinidadian owned Oh ya the new name now in a foreign is Trinidad Air because the Trinity which is the Three dads now own you.

  Yes hey Trinidad a now you fi laugh at wi and rub it in our face and tell us not even Reggae we will have and at the rate the artists are going there will be none.

  Also it's time to tell us we have nothing and wi backawall because you own us and there isn't a damned thing anyone of us can do. A SOCA TIME. BACCHANAL.

  Remember how we the Jamaican's use to show off on you guys now pop style pan wi and shock out because Jamaican WUKLISS. Shock Out because no Jamaican can pop style now. All you have to say is Caribbean Airlines-Trinidad owned. HONESTLY TRINIDAD I AM SO PROUD OF YOU AND THANKFUL. THANK YOU BECAUSE JAMAICAN'S DESERVE THIS.

Everything we have we sell it out then turn around and cry. We don't think of the future of the country nor do we think about the future of our children and grand children. Yes future generations.

- *Bauxite –No longer Jamaican owned*
- *Sugar Company no longer Jamaica owned*
- *Telecommunications so not Jamaican owned*
- *JPS-Privatized –not Jamaican owned*
- *Jamaica itself-not Jamaican owned – see your debt load – US, IMF and World Bank owned-meaning own you*
- *The people well let's put it this way will become slave owned-owned by slave masters once again*

This reminds me of something someone said to me. I do not know if it is true but the person said Seaga said he was going to pack Jamaican's like how dem pack sardine in a sardine tin and after reading about your economy and what is happening in Jamaica I guess the comment is true.

DOES LAMBS GOING TO THE SLAUGHTER HOUSE RING A BELL? THAT'S YOU THE JAMAICAN PEOPLE RIGHT NOW. LAMBS BEING LED TO THE SLAUGHTER HOUSE BECAUSE UNNU WUKLISS.

Seriously though Jamaica where are you headed and how will you support your people in the years to come. Meaning the next 5-10 years if not less? Well its less you guys don't have 5-10 years because doom and gloom looms in 2012.

Do you have a solid future?

How will you survive the great depression to come? This massive earthquake – Tsunami to come.

Suicide rates are on the increase and it will get worse

Your people will be more impoverished meaning the rise is your poverty rate will reach more than 100 percent

Economically your people will suffer

The murder rate will be so out of control that blood will run like river on your island.

Tell me something Jamaica with all that is said will this be "YOUR NEW WORLD ORDER" Did Queen Ifrica and Steele not sing about this new world order and ask the same question?

Jamaicans do you not all say Jamaica is blessed so tell me where is your blessing? Why is Jamaica not blessed today?

Everyone a unno a run to di belly of the beast, the new seat of Babylon and none of you are heading the cry of those that have gone before us when they say "Babylon your throne gone down."

The throne of Babylon is falling on its last leg right now because it must fall and will fall. Trust me there will be worldwide economic disaster because Babylon is broke. Look at their debt load as well.

Babylon must fall and will fall. Yes I wrote the book Saving America From A Woman's Perspective but in the book I told them it is not to save them but to give God's people time to exit Babylon - prolong their eventual downfall .

The blood of the innocent has reached the heavens and it is time for wickedness to return unto to the wicked. Rest assured Jamaica if you don't change your dirty ways in the next couple of months you will come to a timely end because you are so not heeding the call of God.

Jamaica how many hurricanes must touch your land before you wake up?

Port Royal sank over 400 years ago and you have not heeded your lesson?

You recently had a minor earthquake and you still have not heeded the warning. What does it take for you to learn? A brimstone and fiya unnu want? Well keep the crap up and before you know it it will happen. When brimstone and fiya level unno backside maybe then unno will learn. But then if brimstone and fiya level unno wait nothing will be left. Allelujah this is what the people are crying for Jah, Jah Allelujah, Jah this is what they want, fiya and brimstone a wha dem a wuk fa so let it be. Let dem wickedness come back full thrust on them because sey a dat dem tell you dem want.

Jah-God look at the beautiful name you have given them and they have disrespected your name and land more than any other nation. Look pan dem. ***Dem wus dan crab inna barrel.***

Dem no noa sey Jamaica means God made me. They were the first creation. People go back to Genesis and read what it said. God created man out of his own image. You made them. Created them in your likeness hence the name Ja-Mai-Ca-God made me and they disrespect and disgrace your holy land and name.

Coo pan dem God. Coo pan dem. A breed of disgraceful parasites that have forgotten where they came from. Coo pan dem God. Coo pan dem. A bunch of backbiting, obeah working abomination.

Yes Jamaica and Jamaican's mi a cuss unno. Look pan unno. Unnu no deserve the name Jamaica because each and every day you all disrespect it and disrespect God. Look at the beautiful island God has given all of you and each and every day all of you disrespect it.

Come on Jamaica look at where your island is situated. God separated you from the heathens and what have you done? This reminds me of Eve when God told her not to lay with Satan but she committed the sinful act because she was married to Adam and she had sex with him. When she did this God asked her "What have you done?"

Now I ask you Jamaica "WHAT HAVE YOU DONE?"

What have you done?

Jamaica has become the new birthplace of corruption and hunger meaning blood.

When does it all stop?

Right now the island has become a killing field for the wicked

Evil men can murder, behead men and woman, rape, men and women are now bleaching their skin without knowing this is big time disrespect and dishonour in the eyes of God. Trust me none have no part and parcel with God because they are doomed meaning they have condemned their souls to hell. Men are like and are prostitutes, service jockeys as they are so notedly known.

Aids have control of the bedroom because it is so widespread that you don't even know who has it now.

Child slavery-abductions is so rampant that nothing is being done about it and all that is being offered up offered up is a prayer.

Did Baby Cham NOT sing about this - well the murders that has been happening in his song ***Conscience?***

- Did not Peetah Morgan warn you in his song Save the World?

- *Go back to the past*

- Did Marcus Garvey not tell you about enterprise and how to conduct yourself economically?

- Did Bob Marley not educate you on God, your political system?

- Did he not educate you about education?

- D*id he Bob Marley not tell you about the Babylonian system in his song* **_War_**?

- Did he not tell you about the freedom tree?

- Did he Bob Marley not tell you about the Natural Mystic that was in the air in Jamaica?

- Did he not teach you about what it means to be Rasta?

- Did Peter Tosh not educate you on a higher mystical order in **_Rastarfari Is_**

- Did Peter Tosh not try to educate you on your history?

**All these modern day messengers that God gave onto you you the people shot them down because they did not conform to the Babylonian system. A system that Jamaica have embraced and adopted.**

**They were not house slaves like the lot of us**.

Every little thing they did to try and save you you run to massa and carry news. Everything Massa missa so and so a plot this and none of you know that you were screwing yourselves as well as your future in the end.

Now when we want to do something positive for the black community you as blacks complain and say no it will have a negative impact. Den unnu same one complain and sey di system a no fi wi.

Maybe if you stopped to think and stop shooting your own down we will have a positive system for ourselves. We are the ones that don't want to see the black man and black woman rise. We cut our own down, plot to murder them because they see a better future for the black race. God gave them a little insight to make blacks future ready and we kill them.

Stop the damned complaining because good people did try to give us our own school system and we fought against them so suffa in the system that you sell out your own for.

Stop complaining about the system keep us down because we don't elect our own blacks to political office and make them accountable when it comes to representing the black race and the country. *__Meaning that they don't let us hold our head__* *down in shame and none of you look to me because there are blemishes on my record.*

Stop complaining about how you don't eat at black restaurants but then run to every fast food joint to eat the crap they put in the food

Stop complaining about how your children are not learning anything in school because the lot of us meaning some of us as parents, mothers and fathers don't sit down with our children and help them with their homework. *Some fathers don't even accompany mothers to parent teacher interviews but as Sunday day come you si dem dress up in a business suit and briefcase and go worship a Babylonian God.*

We don't teach our children right. We don't teach them not to follow after sin and bad company.

We don't teach them about life

Some of us as parents know we have bad ass children and we turn a blind eye to what they are doing

As parents we don't monitor their face book and twitter accounts. Trust me some of the crap that your sons and daughters post up is amazing. I a

mother and trust me I see because my kids show me and at times I watch what they are doing. Yes I stand over them and trust me they do protest. I cannot see all they do but take a stand these are your children.

I know I am generalizing but for all the parents that do do these things, monitor your children social network, attend parent teach interviews and yes go the extra mile for your children I am sorry because I did not mean to include you.

Yes Jamaica and Jamaicans mi noa sey mi mash unnu caane but a so mi afi do it to get unnu attention. Cuss mi but truss mi mi noa fi cuss to afterall mi a raw bane Jamaican to. Not the spit doa.

Jamaica do you know that you are blessed and highly favoured by God? Out of your island the truth comes. Not Africa but Jamaica and the lot of you are disrespecting the name of God as well as God.

Come now people hold your head up because you are a nation that is blessed. Turn from the state of disarray in now and uphold the name of God-Ja.

Cuss mi now because from the first sentence the warra warra it tan tarra it clate whey mi get.

Some a unnu a sey bet the fossey hole caane come a Jamaica.

Some a unnu a sey shi no affi come mi shi tan dey because wey shi dey wi ave fiwi people dem. Shi no noa what a clack a strike.

Laade some a unnu a sey mi fi go you know what aanda mi madda

Some a unnu the BC and PC dem wey unnu spew only the air and God can tell

Is that all you got. Unnu caane cuss den.

Di draws dem no come down yet and di batty hole dem no show yet?

YES MI TOUCH UNNU, MASH UNNU CAANE DO BETTER AND SECURE THE FUTURE OF JAMAICA BEFORE UNNU GET WIPE OFF THE FACE OF THE PLANET EARTH BECAUSE SEY DESTRUCTION SET FI UNNU AND UNNU NO NOA.

God is securing your asses and every day you spit in his face. I've told you in my other books I have tried praying for you and I vomited big time because your sins have gotten too far out of hand.

You have corrupted and defiled the land and name of God.

You have become a nation of vipers instead of becoming the nation of the blessed. This is it Jamaica because if you don't turn yourself around you will crash and burn. You own nothing. Tell me what do you have to be proud of?

Not even the name of God you have anymore because God will soon flee from you if you don't smarten up.

Look pan wi boonunoonus and sweet island. It's a shame and disgrace what is happening out there.

Learn from Marcus Garvey and stop being so damned lickey lickey. Nuff a unnu have family and friends a foreign and every minute unnu stress wi out. ***Stop stressing us out we have problems too, we have our children we have to feed. What the hell do you think wi pick money off a tree? We work damned hard for it. Just as you are catching your ass down there we are catching our ass up here too.***

We don't have it easy. Do you think it's easy getting up in the winter to go to work? Put your damned hand in a freezer box for a couple of seconds and feel how it's cold. It gets colder up here too. (***People don't literally put your hand in a freezer. I repeat do not put your hand in a freezer).*** You have to realize there is economic distress everywhere. Not because we are here does not mean it is better ***and to some of you Yadi wey go home and brag and show off bout unnu have this and that stop it because some a unnu no ave dry shit in unnu ass. Some a unnu a live wuse dan dog because unnu so riddled in debt that collection agency looking for unnu.***

Stop giving people false hope and stop showing off on what you do not have. Nuff a unnu say unnu drive Benz but cannot pay your rent. Can't even find five dalla fi buy unnu pickney a bag a milk. So how unnu a drive Benz? Ooh a rental.

My people you can cuss me out and laugh at me when I get into hot water. You will say feel it because the table is now turned. Feel it because yu di cuss wi but no matter you need to wake up and smell the coffee.

Come now Jamaica you have so much rich people abroad as well as living on the island and none of them could come together and buy out Air Jamaica?

Honestly mi a wrinch and I am not going to be a hypocrite about it. I am speaking my mind because Jamaica has reached the lowest of the low but I have to be real because we do not take care of our own nor are we proud of our own so what we get now is what we deserve.

A Jamaica dat how di hell wi a go sell it out like dat. What about the future of our children. Wait we don't have a future because the politicians you've elected both Black and White and yes Chinese are like unto the modern day Judas. Sell us out for dirty pieces of silver. And we that are living abroad are no different because we too allow this to happen. We need a voice that is heard and heeded. We cannot say we love our country, proud to be a Jamaican when shit like this is happening in our born land. God took us out of Africa to a new land. To his land. Ja-Mai-Ca the land where he made us. This is the land of creation but none of you know this. It's time we hold up our heads and build our land not through violence but through smarts, economic stability.

It's time to vote out the corrupt officials and clean up the land so that we can stand proud and say yes this is the Jamaica God need. If you can't vote them out make them accountable for the mess they have created. Cut their pay. Do not pay them let them pay back the money they got to help the community. No if they cannot represent you and your community in a positive manner let that elected official pay the government back the money it gave them including their salaries. Come on now. Do better now.

WE CANNOT CHANGE JAMAICA WITH VIOLENCE BUT THROUGH ECONOMIC REFORM. WE NEED TO GO BACK TO THE BOOKS OF MARCUS MOSIAH GARVEY. He did tells us that there are two forms of blacks the regressive and the progressive as clearly put by him Marcus Mosiah Garvey. *The regressive blacks you can take them so far and if they are not willing to learn kick them off your coat tail because they are the ones to hold you down and hold you back in life and we cannot afford this anymore. The progressive black is always thinking ahead, always moving forward and it is* _time for us as blacks to move forward. Become progressive and stop being regressive._

We have to start thinking and doing as progressive people. We cannot sit down and expect a handout.

We are creative people _**AND I AM DAMNED PROUD TO BE A JAMAICAN. I DON'T CARE HOW BROKE WE GET I AM DAMNED PROUD BECAUSE I KNOW THE PROTENTIAL OF MY OWN PEOPLE. IF WE CAN HAVE A BOBSLED TEAM THAT MADE IT SO FAR IN THE WINTER GAMES WE CAN RECOVER AND OWN AIR JAMAICA AS WELL AS TAKE BACK WHAT IS RIGHTFULLY OURS.**_

We can no longer let our politician's rape us of our future. We as Jamaican's can no longer rape ourselves of our future because right now _**YOU ARE ON THE BRINK OF STARVATION, THE BRINK OF ECONOMIC AND ENVIRONMENTAL COLLAPSE.**_

Currently Jamaica is _**BROKE**_. It will default on its loans and then chaos will be unleashed on the island.

We cannot sit and wait and lay in ignorance and not see what is going on around us. We have to do something before chaos happens.

We are people that have a voice and please do not pick up violence to let your voice be heard because this is civilized times.

We need to elect officials that have the best interest of Jamaica and the Jamaican people at heart.

These people we elect you as people have to hold them accountable for your life because you are electing them to not make you as a people and country suffer in hard times.

That means if they start with the bullshit vote them the hell out of office immediately by calling for an early election and vote them out. ***None of us as Jamaican's can say we love the country and ourselves and rape BEAUTIFUL JAMAICA LIKE THIS. COME ON NOW JAMAICA SWEETER THAN CHOCOLATE TEA AND YOU KNOW HOW CHOCOLATE TEA SWEET AND SMELL NICE.***

Jamaica God went so far as kept his name Ja with you and all of you including me is telling

God we don't want it. We don't want his land. People are we BC stupid. ***WI AVE GOD NAME NO ADDA COUNTRY CAN SAY THIS BUT WE CAN. WE SHOULD BE DAMNED PROUD OF THIS BUT YET WE ARE SHOWING THE WORLD THAT WE DON'T CARE AND WE ARE NOT PROUD.***

JAMAICA IS THIS LOVE?

DO WE TRULY LOVE JAMAICA?

WI NO CARE BOUT IT

Go to your internet and pull us 'THIS IS LOVE" BY J. BOOG AND MONSTRA and here what they say about true love and if we truly love Jamaica we need to change and save our land.

TRUST IN GOD MY PEOPLE TO GET US OUT OF THIS. WHEN HE GETS US OUT LET US STAY OUT OF OUR MESS AND PROVE TO THE WORLD THAT WE ARE TRULY THANKFUL TO GOD BECAUSE HE TOOK US FROM NOWHERE TO SOMEWHERE. Meaning God took us out of our mess and stayed the destruction that is to come.

IF WE MAKE JAMAICA FALL WE CANNOT BLAME ANYONE BUT OURSELF BECAUSE WE ALL CAN SAVE JAMAICA AND BRING IT BACK FROM THE BRINK OF DESTRUCTION. THIS I KNOW.

**Like I said and will forever say I want and need Jamaica to feel it worse than any country because God has blessed us with his name**

**He's given us people that teach and preach to us, people that tell us how we should conduct ourselves and we are not listening.**

**We give up the right way for the wrong way and now it is too late.**

LISTEN YOU DON'T HAVE TO LIKE ME.

SHIT YOU CAN CUSS AND HATE ME ALL YOU WANT BUT THE FINAL BELL TOLLS FOR YOU AND I WILL REPEAT AND TELL YOU THIS OVER AND OVER AGAIN.

YU SI DAT LIKKLE EARTHQUAKE WEY UNNU GET. DAT A PRELUDE FOR BIGGER THINGS TO COME AND IT IS BREWING TRUSS MI ON DAT. YU TINK MI A GO HALLA FI YU.

Do you think I am going to cry for you?

Mi try pray fi unnu an mi vomit and it's not one time I tried to pray for you. So think because enough is enough. Truly enough is enough.

You cannot rear your children to commit wickedness

You cannot hide the truth from your children anymore

You cannot sit there and think God will send you a saviour to save you. Well no I *rephrase that because I am writing this book and no I am not your saviour.*

Mi truly love Jamaica mi no love di people. No dat a lie mi truly love di people mi jus no love unnu dirty and corrupt ways.

I've told you in another of my books that I saw the three angels of God in my dream descending from the Southwest of Jamaica. People these are God's angels coming down. I did not see them in any other land. Jamaica is privileged and you are taking away your future. These are the angels of God people.

Wey unnu a tell God sey.

Unnu a tell God unnu want his angels to come into a dirty land. Well let me tell you something they will not come if Jamaica continues with its dirty ways.

Your house, you the people, your country have to be clean. Remember I told you I asked God to come into my home and he told me my house was dirty. He could not come in and it is time we clean our house, clean up our island or we will miss the call of God. We will miss our salvation, our time to be with God in his holy temple.

And Jamaica I will always mass your corn not because I hate you but because I truly love you and want what is best for you. You don't have to like me but do better for yourself and I am going to suggest some things to help you get back on track. I do not know if they will work but look into them because this is your future.

You need to think and help yourself.

Jamaica my sweet sweet Jamaica no other land compares to you

You are the birthplace of creation

The one that now houses the truth

The land that houses true life

Life has come home

Receive it

Cherish it

Never let it go again

Live Up to your name

Your holy and divine name

Teach your children about it so that when the angels come they can hold their head up and be proud to call themselves Ja-Mai-Cans because this was the land where God made them as well as made you.

Be proud my people because ***OUT OF MANY ONE PEOPLE.***

As for the Rasta's I told you you cannot put Ethiopia over your own land because Ethiopia disgraced God. Ethiopia turned from God so why are you turning to people that knows no respect for God.

- They are a walking abomination unto God.

- And Ethiopians none of you can dispute this. You all know the truth of your origin hence you speak the devil's tongue. Practice the religion of the devil hence you were put in the bible as a testament of what we should not become. And Jamaicans – Rastas that is. Know the truth and live. You cannot wear the crown without knowing how to represent it. You all claim to have higher knowledge then I suggest you use it. I could throw parables at you but I refuse to. Read into what I am saying and know what I am saying. Like I said you all say you have higher learning use it because what I have given you above none of you can say is nothing. If you do then you don't know the truth nor do you have higher learning. You will all be frauds and I will not take back what I said. You should know the truth in words.

- Ethiopia do you know how much God loved you?

- Do you know how much God protected you?

- Cherished you

- God favoured you so much and you spat in his face just like we the Jamaican's are doing today.

- Rasta's' break away and love up your land and do not make it become desolate like Ethiopia. You can hate me for this and what I write but I do not care because you too lukewarm but do not have the full truth.

- You cannot say you wear the crown

- Wear the garb of honour

- You cannot profess to be Ras and pollute your way

- You cannot let your women and men pollute themselves

- You cannot teach your children from pagan doctrines and say it is of God

- You cannot take up the unholy ways of pagans and say it is God's way

- You cannot say you are Ethiopian Orthodox and pick up the cross because the cross is associated with and is a part of Babylonian – pagan customs

Look at Jamaica because it is out of your land that the full truth is coming out of.

Tell me something what has Ethiopia done for Jamaica and its people?

What is Ethiopia doing for Jamaica now?

You have God's name

You wear the CROWN OF GOD'S ANGELS – meaning you have the hair because it is this hair that I see God's angels with time and time again

One of your colours are off but you will figure it out. Just take out the red because this colour is not associated with God per say, yes it's a warning colour but red is not a colour that is worn by the angels I saw descending on your land. Add one more colour from your flag. Not the black. Now you have and know the true colours of God. Meaning these three colours are the colours I saw the angels wearing when they were walking on the land in Jamaica. This is also the colours I saw Morgan Heritage wearing because the sceptre of knowledge did pass to them but they do not know this. Let's put it this way they have lost their way because I no longer see them in these colours anymore.

Morgan Heritage you can cuss all you want but I am telling you like I saw it in my dream. Bob Marley's children did not get the sceptre to carry on the truth in music you did because Bob's children still do not know the magnitude of this man's spiritual power. Until this day they do not know.

LET ME PUT IT IN ALL CAPS AND BOLD IT FOR THE WORLD TO KNOW AND READ.

UNTIL THIS DAY THEY DO NOT KNOW. THEY DON'T KNOW THAT BOB MARLEY THEIR FATHER IS CALLED KING CHARO IN THE SPIRITUAL WORLD.

No one that I know of or ever read about when I was younger ever got this honour meaning was named king in the spiritual world. I read about Elijah and heard about him ascending directly to heaven but none was ever called king accept for this man.

Some of you are saying this is impossible and can never happen well I am educating you and telling you it did happen because this was what I saw in my vision. This man relayed to me, told to me in my vision and I am telling you. In the spiritual realm he is called King Charo. I do not know how to spell the name and this is the best I can do. As to the origin of the name I do not know.

Jamaica ROBERT NESTA MARLEY came out of your land and is called King Charo in the spiritual realm and you are still jerking around with your country and music.

Marcus Mosiah Garvey came out of your land meaning he was born in Jamaica and you are still jerking around with your country and your future.

Peter Tosh came out of your land and you are still jerking around with your country and your history

- *You have the truth so why are you living by lies?*

- *Why are you searching elsewhere for the truth when you have it?*

- *You have the truth in your country's name*

- *You have the truth inside of you*

- *You have the truth coming out of your land*

- ***Your people have the crown of glory***

- ***The garb of honour***

- ***The music***

Why are you throwing it away for something else?

Rasta's you cannot let unholy people represent you by wearing your crown of glory and polluting it. I've told you this already and none of you are listening.

You have to live as Jamaican's. God's people because you are from God.

Made by God

You know how holy and blessed Ethiopia was

Did you know Ethiopia had a holy man that could control the elements? Meaning the weather but they turned from God by walking on his holy ground with their shoes. For further clarity I asked this man in my dream why does God hate Ethiopians because I read it in the bible that God hated Ethiopians and would make the land desolate and he showed me his shoes. He did not tell me he showed me.

So Rasta's why are you holding Ethiopia in high esteem if you know that they dishonoured God in this way

The crown of God Selassie did not wear so why are you posing him up?

Educate me on this

I know why Ethiopia was mentioned in the bible. It's not just about the shoes there is significantly more to it and I have covered it in another book.

Know your history. Know who you are because as it is you are all following a lost cause. You are Jamaican which stands for God Made Me. Jah Made Me so why are you following the Ethers.

Meaning the people of the gaseous clouds. Yes some people associate Ether to your hair but they don't have your hair.

Yes some of you Rasta scholars can jar at me but guess what I do not follow the pagan system of things you do because none of you know your true history nor why Ethiopia was put in the bible. None of you know the significance of a countries name or the significance of symbolism because if you did you wouldn't be whoring and begging to become a part of another man's land.

Dig further in his history and you will know the full truth.

Dig deeper and you will know that Selassie was so not from the tribe of Judah and make no mistake I will be clarifying Judah and Israel later on in another book. He could never have been. Yes you can hate me and call me demented but the truth is there you just don't want to know. None of you respect Jah because if you did you would respect Ja-Mai-Ca.

You would know what your land represent. You would know how powerful the name is and what it represents and you would truly Jamaica not just love it.

If God hates Ethiopia and God does not hate people I asked the question using hate and I got the answer. So if God hates Ethiopia why are you posing them up and do not tell me because Ethiopia is mentioned Genesis because the Babylonians had to put that in there. Meaning they had to add Ethiopia there and trust me I know the reason why and yes it will be outlined in another book and stop saying typical.

None of us know our history or heritage and this is sad.

We take up books of men and say yes it is divinely inspired and ***NONE OF YOU KNOW THAT THESE BOOKS ARE BASED A WATERED DOWN VERY WATERED DOWN VERSIONS OF OUR HERITAGE. BLACK HERITAGE AND HISTORY AND YES HINDU HISTORY.***

TELL ME SOMETHING BLACK PEOPLE HOW CAN THESE BOOKS BE DIVINELY INSPIRED WHEN IT IS OUR OWN STORY BEING TOLD TO US. AND YES BEING SOLD TO US.

CONFUSED

READ THE BIBLE AGAIN AND KNOW ¼ OF YOUR HISTORY.

- Know the truth and comprehend it so that we are no longer enslaved again and trust me at the rate we are going we will be enslaved again. Infinitely trust me on this.

If you think the slavery we went through in Egypt and some parts of the West is anything like that is to come think again. Trust me infinitely when I tell you this it is going to be worse because the devil and his people will not dick around. White people if you are reading this book you are not and will not be immune to this. Your ass will cry like a bitch too.

- All of you will cry but this time around no one will save you because you sold God out.

- Jamaicans just take a look at Air Jamaica. You sold AIR GOD OUT TO THE THREE DADS – YES THE TRINITY.

- You know not what the six pointed star represent. Many of you are pointing downwards. Why point the triangle down. You're not dead point it up. Live up and elevate yourself. What are you telling me you love to live down? You love to bow down to the dead. If you don't know the truth of the triangle don't showcase it because the triangle is not for the lot of you. Don't just wanna be Know. If you know the full truth of the triangle then showcase it if not step off.

- You know not what life is or how life originated but yet you claim. Don't just claim know and BE.

- You do not know how the universe was created or who created it

- You know not how we came upon the face of the planet

- You know absolutely nothing about life in the spiritual realm and trust me you do not need weed or the use of weed to get you there. Now you can cuss me out but I stand by my words.

- You do not need to meditate to have a connection with God and this you do not know because God is connected to you and as Bob told you **if you listen very carefully you will hear. Meaning sit quietly and pray you will see and hear God**

- You have the music yes

- The language you do not have and no one on the face of the planet have the language meaning we cannot speak it but a handful can write it but do not comprehend the scope of it because they cannot heal people with it nor can they drive away evil with it.

- And Rasta's no language on the face of this planet come close to it but you should know this because some of you talk about the seventh seal

- You know the importance of the seventh seal and all of you should know that no man on the face of this planet can break it because the seventh seal was never entrusted to a man but a woman

- You can laugh and say this is ludicrous because you all believe in the Trinity so therefore you are not of God because God is not a trinity nor is he the three dads. Now put it together if you have right and absolute knowledge.

- Let me educate you on God. In the physical realm God is a female but in the spiritual realm God is male and if you know the full truth of Adam and Eve in the beginning then you would know the full truth about Ethiopia – yes the mother land

- Do not comprehend. Take a look at the male gene. See it and know it.

- *Know and not just believe because it is through knowledge that you will enter into God's abode which is not heaven.*

  Everything is in your genes you should know this hence the word Genesis. The genes is and you cannot change this nor can you change the truth.

  Yes man is trying to change this but no matter how you manipulate the genes you cannot change it because in time it will revert back to the truth and this man do not know. I repeat you cannot change the genes hence we have interracial children.

  Figure it out if you have higher knowledge. And no it is not wrong to have bi-racial children. Was not Bob Marley Bi-racial and you all love and adore him.

- Trust me there is a heaven but heaven is in the afterlife and this is not where God resides.

- Heaven is just a temporary resting place and this you need to know

- Life moves forward unto greater knowledge and truth. Knowledge and truth that our mind cannot comprehend in our physical state. It's like I've stated and will forever tell you there is light in the darkness but the naked eye cannot see it. Further this light is hard to detect with the spiritual eye. Meaning we cannot see the light because our spirituality is not fully developed.

- Many of you know the cradle of life and where it begins

- Many of you know that the brain is the heart and not the heart as we know it

- Many of you know about Melchezidec but none of you know the full truth about him

- Many of you know him as having no mother or father but we know everything must have a mother and father

- Many of you know the importance of nature and how important it is to keep mind body and soul pure but many of you are not living by the truth nor are you living by the pureness of life because many of you disrespect your wives, your husbands and yes Jah

- Many of you still believe in false doctrines and practice them

- Some of you eat pork

- Some of you still have wife at home and have a lover down the street and this goes for the women as well

- There is unity in numbers and there is a lot of Rasta's across the globe of different nationality and none of you know the full truth and none of you bring racism into this because there is no racism where God resides

- God does not hate based on colour but he sure as hell can hate you for the wickedness and evil that you have done so none of you get it twisted because the Garden of Eden did not house Blacks alone. White people resided in the Garden of Eden as well because that is how I saw it in the past. Take a look at the picture of the Ying and Yang and you will know the full truth in life and yes in death. Meaning it represents life in the physical and life in the spiritual and so much more but none of you can comprehend the scope of its knowledge. And people let no one tell you that you cannot dream in the past because you can. It is not a frequent thing but it does happen. Yes I am repeating myself too because I told you this in another book.

And Rasta's I am going to stop here because I am repeating myself from my previous book.

As for you Jamaica and Jamaicans you know about the dead, you know if you listen carefully you can hear the dead cry like a bitch in the grave. Jamaicans you know the dead walk and interfere with life and it's no obeah crap so let no one tell you that the dead hath no power because all of you know that evil hath a lot of power.

I know you die hard Christian's are laughing and saying I am lying and to you I send you to Job where God was talking to Satan.

Yes people God was talking to Satan read it again.

God said to Satan "have you considered my servant Job?" Read further to where it said "God told Satan to do all he can to Job but do not what?"

Yes "take his life" now you know that evil can take life and create havoc in your life so stop saying that evil has no power because you know evil hath power.

Jamaica as for you and saving yourself these are my suggestions and I know how ingenious we can be, meaning think of the bobsled team.

Jamaica is a hot country that is located in the Caribbean Sea and we had a Bobsled team. We don't get snow. Forget the mountains people. We do not get sub zero temperatures.

If a man can build a motorcycle out of lawn mowers what are we saying for ourselves?

If you can do this then hey we can do anything

University science students yes you Mr. UWI student I told China about dung how about trying to make fuel from human and animal waste. This also means we will no longer have to dump our poop poop in the sea and ocean. Seas and Oceans were we get fish from. Fish we consume.

We grow corn and sugar cane these can be used to make clean and reliable fuel why not use them to make your own fuel instead of relying on the oil and crude oil of the East

Jamaican's abroad I am coming to you. Many of us have been educated in Engineering – Renewable Energy. We work for others and bitch about it. How about going home and setting up shop

Currently Jamaican's cannot afford their electric bills many of you know about Solar Energy and Wind Technology the Caribbean right now is ripe and need a change. Take into consideration the climate changes that are occurring meaning the glaciers are depleting and if the ice continues to melt away what about earth's water supply so think. We use water for electricity plus other means and remember I did tell you Renewable Energy is the way to go because it was given to me in a vision so capitalize on this while the market is ripe. Hey once you have the market in Jamaica and the Caribbean expand to Africa because no one is thinking about Africa and capitalizing on Africa. Everyone thinks the resources in Africa is being drained and there is no money there but let them think that way because you now know otherwise. Hey once we set up shop in Africa and I am going to be racist here people. Once we start developing Africa and restore it back to pristine purity we can say to those racist bastards that keep telling us to get out of their country to get the F out of Africa. We can say Africa is for African so now develop the motherland and make God and his angels proud.

Africa know your people and if we want to come back and develop Africa do not stop your people. And black people be forewarned the same shit you carry out in the West do not take it into Africa. Respect the Motherland, respect your colour and do not rape the country. If you truly love to create or build do it out of true love and not love.

Love deceives but true love can never deceive. And the whoredom must stop. Do not take a wife in the motherland knowing full well you are married to someone in the West. Do this shit and trust me infinitely I will petition God to turn back your evil unto to you. The F---ry has to stop.

So be forewarned because if I die before all of you I will make your life and anyone that tries to mess up Africa I will make your life, your children's life and your future generations life a living nightmare because none will see or inherit the beauty of any African Kingdom whether in Africa or anywhere in the universe and beyond where black people reside. This I give you my solemn word on.

Stop raping your people

We've been raped of everything by other nations and yes our own long enough. Stop the nonsense now man. Enough is enough.

I don't care what reasoning you have it stops now.

Jamaican's you can do something too

How many producers do you have out there?

Some of the music that is coming out of Jamaica is so crappy that I don't even want to listen to it and trust me people I can get off on some of you female artist but I will refrain because NONE A DEM A GOODDAS DEM A PROSTITUE. Nuff a dem a sell dem poakey fi bread and pad.

IF UNNU POAKEY SO GOOD WEY MAN A FI PAY DUNG PAN IT FA? UNNU NO FI AVE DI MAN LOCK. IF UNNU A GOODAS A MAN WILL KNOW HIS PLACE THAT HE SHOULD CONTRIBUTE TO THE HOUSEHOLD, HELP RAISE THE KIDS AND VISE VERSA.

Your man should be outlining YOUR POAKEY with Diamonds and Pearls. Everyday im gaane a work he should be rushing home to it and not stop off at sister Pat for a quick touch up before he comes home to you and give you the what lef – the leftovers.

Look at some of you, unnu a glorify yourself and unnu done and look wus dan a dam waste chute. And for many of you that don't know what a waste chute is it is something you throw your garbage down. *RESPECT YOUR DAMNED SELF IT GOES A LONG WAY.*

Hey mi throw mi caane mi no call no fowl so if anyone of you pick it up then the caane ketch the right fowl.

As for you men that use the women as target practice stop it because it could be your sister. We all came from a mother stop using your penis or dick for golf practice because the sex some of you give is not all that. 30 seconds to 2 minutes if that some of you give and think that is something - you are all that.

The best sex anyone can have is spiritual sex and trust me once you've had that you don't want anything else so none of you are worth shit. It is that good. It is so good that you don't want none of your sorry asses because what you give is crap.

Having a donkey cubby means nothing once you've had spiritual sex. White people some of you call these wet dreams because you have an organism in the spiritual and physical realm at the same time. All the motions you are going through in the spiritual you are going throw them in the physical.

And Jamaican's a no duppy sin ting because mi noa the duppy thing.

Now that I have that out of the way and once again I have become target practice for every Jamaican male and female let me continue.

We need to create entrepreneurs in Jamaica. I know you have entrepreneurs already by how sustainable are they on a global economic scale?

How many of them can you find listed in Forbes Magazine? See where I am going with this?

Jamaican's we cannot say we have tourism and bauxite when we do not own a bauxite company.

We do not have a National Airline so how does this help our economy. It's not helping Jamaica it's helping other countries.

Many of you are saying employment. Many of us are employed by these companies. True but where does the money go? Is the money not taken out of the country because the parent company is located elsewhere so how does this benefit Jamaica when the money is leaving your country and these companies can leave the country at any time?

Tell me something Jamaica how do you run out of sugar? Now mi a go inna Bashment Granny and quote granny when the father is telling his son this. "YU WUKLISS"

Jamaica unnu wukliss. You produce sugar grow the damned cane so how the hell do you run out of sugar.

When I was growing up I remembered Mr. Brown making wet sugar. He made it himself so why can't you make it yourself. Forget the length of time you are just being damned lazy. We use to use rock stone and beat the cane then ring it to get its juice. Why couldn't you do that? Wukliss.

You are so damned commercialized that you are willing to starve, go hungry instead of doing things the old fashioned way when things are scarce. _**That's why I love farmers because they know the times to reap and the times to sow. A conscious farmer could never go hungry or be hungry. If he did, it would be carelessness on his part.**_

Panganat – Pomegranate grows wild down there. Many of you use it to play kick ball. None of you know that it is good for the blood and heart. Grow it and sell it to other countries.

Let your Minister of Agriculture do his damned job and start marketing Jamaica's assets.

Weed still grow it organically. Jamaica has the best weed in the world. Yes I am being biased can't help it. Strike a deal with pharmaceutical companies and sell them your weed.

Come on now the Ganja farmer dey bout help im to no man

Other countries produce and sell plants associated with narcotics. Make it legal now.

Sorrel is also good for the heart combine Pomegranate and Sorrel and make heart healthy juices. Sell them in the Caribbean and abroad - foreign

Gunman lade have mercy but I am going to mash unnu caane. Mi a go step pan unnu toe but you are the next one.

Tell me something how much duppy you need?

Do you not know that one duppy brings your soul into hell because the blood of the innocent cries out night and day to God?

Think because the life you take here in the physical has you locked in the spiritual and there will be no escaping hell - yes the judgment.

The senseless violence have to stop.

Mi mi Michelle a tell unnu say none a unnu a bad man or Dan because a true bad man no tek life and run. Dem tan up and face the penalty. The man wey tan up a true bad man. Him a Dan, im no run from police. Some a unnu hide behine oman like Osama. Him a pancoote only pancoote run and hide. The wickedest man and the badest man to walk this planet a Satan because im ave wi lock inna di physical and spiritual. None a unnu no bad like him. Him a di true Dan because he has every nation on the face of this planet doing his bidding. Im a use unnu and none a unnu no noa.

Unnu a tek life and do tek life why run. Tan up.

Stop letting the devil use you. Turn your life around for the better. Think of Jamaica and what you are doing to it. You are hindering her progress.

Why should Jamaica be the murder capital of the world?

Is it not bad enough that every nation meaning race on the face of the planet hate us? Look into it. Truly take a minute to reflect. Now tell me why are we giving them more ammunition to continue to hate us?

I know I have just entered your hit list but mi na run the truth must be heard and told. A true man or woman stands up and face the consequences of his or her actions.

If I do wrong and I am not saying I don't do wrong because I do and when my time come to fall I have to take it as a woman.

Why would I run and hide. I talk the talk so I better stand up and walk the F---ing walk.

My boat will be rocked because I will be on every hit list across the globe but I still have to do my job until my time come when I join the likes of

Moses, Bob Marley, Marcus Garvey, Martin Luther King Jr., Peter Tosh and those before me.

You too Mr. Badman can prosper but how do you prosper?

Turn your ideas into an enterprise but you have to eliminate the killing. Stop the killing. It's not you alone that want to live. Everyone wants to live. Think. Listen to Misty Morning by Duane Stephenson. Love his conscious music. He's cute too. Just had to say that people.

Many of you own the weed market I am just saying.

How many employees do you have?

What if Jamaica is successful in getting contracts from multinational pharmaceutical companies?

Where is your economic portfolio?

Do you have a company to say I am going to set up shop?

How will you fund this?

Do you have a plan of action to take to the bank?

Right now you are struggling and smuggling. Come up with an economic plan of action and keep soliciting your government.

Do you see where I am going with this? The government isn't coming to you go to him but not with violence but with economic smarts.

You need to sustain your future but do it the honest and clean way and always remember once you start up and have the contract there will be more players in the game. Do not eliminate them but up your game? Look at hemp to produce clothes, hey shoes if you have to. Look at alternative means.

How many shoe factories do you have in Jamaica?

We have so much Bamboo trees that we do not know what to do with them and please do not cut down the trees in fern gully. It is a tourist attraction and I want to lose myself in it meaning I want to be marvelled at it at all time. So stay out of Fern Gully. Protect it and truly love it.

How about using the Bamboo to make tables, funky wicker chairs and baskets

Use the Bamboo to make beds and wacked out and innovative headboards

Use the Bamboo to make 3 wheeler bicycles for tourist to discover the island

Come on Jamaicans see with me here as my brain in reeling with ideas for the Bamboo. We have to be innovative like I've said. Everything we have has been sold so do something to help yourself.

Mr. Bad Man your violent ways has and have hurt the country's economy. Your killings as well as the killings you do on a daily basis have had a negative impact on the financial growth of the country. Don't think your killings have had a positive impact on Jamaica. It hasn't.

Many of us bane ya want to return home but the island is marred with so much violence that many of us refuse to step foot back there.

The killings of returnees is not good come on now.

We work hard inna ice box some of us to say we are going to return home when we retire and when we do come home you rob and kills us.

Think people. When returnees come home we employ people because some things we cannot do nor can we withstand the heat so that's money in someone's pocket right there.

When you kill us that income is gone so who's suffering?

Think we employ a lot of people, people that will now contribute to the growth of the island's economy because they now have jobs.

The violence also hurt tourism too. Cash needed by your government to pay people as well as pay back its loans to the IMF and World Bank.

The violence hurts everyone on a whole because money is being taken away from local businesses and with dwindling tourism your unemployment rate goes up. Think of the layoffs in the market place.

People Jamaica is not all bad. There are good people on the island as well as beautiful places to see. Right now I am pleading with the people that are bringing down Jamaica to stop. I need true peace and harmony on the land of Jamaica so it can prosper and its people do not suffer in anguish. Trust me something is brewing for the island and it is not good. I have to cry for peace and try and save the island and them. There is truth in my love and in my words for this island. God knows and know how much I have pleaded for them but I cannot plea anymore. I now have to step aside and let them now see the errors of their ways. I cannot petition God anymore lest he be angry at me. I care too much for the people and it truly hurt me to see my own behaving this way. God if only they knew. If only.

Sean Paul, Shaggy, Morgan Heritage and yes you too Bounty Killer you have a damned big mouth put your mouth to use. You are intelligent but you don't use your intelligence wisely. Stop dissing and arguing over the past it is beneath you because the circle you run in you can get the crème du la crème of them all.

Shit pum pum is bought and sold as a commodity in your circle and you know what I mean by that.

Respect and elevate yourself and if you come and say you are going to diss me in a song be forewarned my pen is hotter.

Stop saying you are the poor people them governor or whatever you say because if you were you would be advocating for the poor and so far you are bag a mouth and chat nothing else.

Say a word and all I got to say is Shaggy Save A Life. Look at the great work he is doing for the children of Bustamante Hospital.

He's stepping up to the plate what are you doing?

What are the rest of the artist doing?

I don't hear about what you are doing to contribute to Jamaica in a positive way.

What are you doing to help the needy?

How many laptops or computers have you donated – given to the schools in the area that you grew up in?

How many pens, pencils and books have you bought and given to a school in need?

Any artist take this up and say they are going to diss Bounty and record a CD on my tirade on Bounty be well advised and forewarned that the pens and pencils will come out on your ass. I did not give any of you any ammunition to go after him or diss him. People any artist that diss Bounty do not buy their CD's. Ban them from your musical catalogue because this is between Bounty and Me and I did not call no damn fowl. In this case Chicken Back. Meaning people that ride on my back my coat tail.

Yes I am on your case Mr. Bounty Killer because there is something about you that I like. Don't know what it is maybe it's the fact that you have so much potential but not using that potential to benefit the people that you say you love and hold in high esteem. Now that I have vented on you listen and yes shut your mouth. And no you caane bax mi dung. And stop calling me names because I am not calling you names. You guys are multi-millionaires follow me here and see if this could work. I am sure the lot of you have a couple million US in your bank account.

In the video tell me how come by Morgan Heritage it showcased areas in Jamaica that are so poverty stricken that it makes you want to cry.

I am not out there so I do not know if people reside in some of these areas. *But if people do not reside there* how about buying the land and make Luxury Condominiums. Revamp these areas and cater to the upper middle class and elite.

Also make affordable condominiums for the poorer class.

Keep in consideration the environment by planting trees and flowers in these communities and please make them different from the housing schemes.

Lord have mercy your housing schemes look so much like the ghetto.

Sorry people but all the houses are the same.

There is no variety. The houses are ugly butt ugly.

Some of you need to fire your architect because they have no appreciation for art and beauty.

Who the hell want to live in the same house that looks exactly like their neighbours?

Boring tasteless and tacky. For real and don't get upset at me just take a drive and look at some of them. Truly take a look. No thought went into designing and building these schemes. Yes I know Jamaica has some beautiful homes but revamp the housing schemes. Stop buying the same old same old be innovative and classy.

__Maybe my ideas are ridiculous to some of you but where I lack knowledge expand on it and always remember it will take time, money and patience. You will have many hurdles in the ways. You have the money expand your horizons.__

Jamaica you have so many things, options at your fingertips capitalize on them. I know it all takes money but if you are lacking money work from home.

Kids do you want to make money?

How about some of you tutor other kids that are lagging behind in school?

Charge $20.00 per hour. I know some kids can't afford the $20.00. Use your bartering skills. Maybe student X is good in science and you are not. Trade your services and take sex out of your mind too damned filthy. Student X is good in science and bad in English let him or her tutor you in Science and you tutor him or her in English. That's bartering.

I've covered this topic in another book I know but you know me Ms. Repeat herself like a broken record.

Jamaican's abroad some of us have money. How about investing in Jamaica? Some of us are retired athletes that were successful. Most months you are not doing anything how about setting up work camps in Jamaica for the youths. Even if it is just for two weeks and go teach them.

Dentist and Doctors do the same. Some of you Dentists up here can volunteer two weeks of your time to a local Hospital or Church.

Doctors you can do the same. Currently the some of the doctors are ill equipped. Meaning they lack knowledge and expertise.

Let's put it this way some doctors are over dosing patients and don't know it.

Some perform C sections and are cutting the baby.

It's not everywhere but it is happening so some of you need to educate them. And Jamaica don't just take any and any doctors in the country. Before they are allowed in make sure that they are accredited. Do your homework with that country's Medical Association in regards to licence revoked, accreditation like I've said, years of practice. Do not just take anyone because many people will come into your country under fraudulent means. I repeat do your homework.

Not because we are not in Jamaica does not mean that we cannot help and do something.

I know safety is the issue for a lot of you so Jamaican's you will now see this. Meaning new faces wanting to come and help, lend a helping hand. Don't kill the people or stress them out. They are doing something good for your children. They are giving them hope. Returnee's the same rule applies as above in Africa. Lose the bullshit it is not necessary because money does not make you better than the next man. Money cannot buy you life. You of all people know one day you have it and the next you don't.

Remember Jamaican's don't ramp if you have forgotten and what no catch quakoo must ketch shirt.

Jamaica you cannot depend on tourism alone because many people cannot afford the cost of a plane ticket so you have to expand your horizon.

Try to get in on the energy market by encouraging people to plant more corn and sell your corn to energy companies in the US and Brazil. They use corn to produce ethanol which is a cleaner way to make fuel and it is good for the environment.

UWI students Coal is a driving force in electrical energy – electricity. I know it emits carbon dioxide but the gases can be trapped. How about finding ways to trap theses gases to make Freon or coolants that are not harmful to the environment?

Can sulphur be added to Coal to make the gas more environmentally friendly?

Do you see where I am going with this?

I am not educated in Science or Chemistry but could we do something with Coal to lessen the toxic emissions in the earth's atmosphere. I don't know if we could mix coal with something so that when it emits CO_2 it has a cooling effect somehow and with this cooling effect it helps in reducing global warming in a positive way.

I know this is beyond my scope. If corn is a plus when it comes to toxic emissions, how do we merge the two? Meaning use coal and corn together or coal and sugar cane and take coal to a new height and keep in mind I do not know anything about Renewable Energy and my ideas are a little wacked. You are the ones with the knowledge meaning you know what can and cannot work.

For all the bed and breakfast joints on the island you have to start marketing yourself. Some of us folks when we come home we want to have a quiet get away. Cater to us with a clean and safe environment. The wicker chairs. Put them on the balcony so we can sit and watch the night sky. Attract us to your community but the community must be safe. Some of us just want those two days to go buck wild in the bedroom with our husband.

Network with fellow community members that have a bar or shop and work something out and please leave greed where it belongs outside. You are working together as a community so the outdoing and cheating shit has to stop. Everyone need to make a dollar you alone cannot have it all. Too damned greedy.

Musicians unnu wukliss to. The lot of you have money and none of you are equipping your homes with solar panels or investing in wind technology. Unnu still a pay fi light bill. Who the hell is managing unnu money? I sure would love to because you're all wukliss. Get future ready. Truss mi I would like to manage some of you and knock some senses into the lot of you.

Unnu palava palava inna Benz, BMW's and Lexus and none of you thought about the future. Equip your homes with solar panels and come off the electrical grid.

Figet the expensive liquor well no that's your fun.

Many of you have been out of commission for decades. Start looking into producing African artists. Belize has some great artist feature some of them. Canada has some up and coming artist as well like Jongo, Cujo, Bassie, Legends like Leroy Brown, Leroy Sibbles work with them.

Take African music to the next level and do not change them from their style by saying these artists have to sing reggae. Capitalize on the language and the music that they have and when the time is right infuse the two. Make a different type of music.

Look to radio stations in Canada like CHRY105.5 FM

G98.7 FM

International artists make yourselves more readily available and use these two radio stations to promote your new music as well.

You can't ignore them. CHRY105.5 FM have done so much for the black community. I don't care if they are a community radio they have more than done there share to promote reggae music. Every genre of music because it is a cultural radio station and I am proud of them.

Sean Paul you promote a lot and you have friend here in Canada pay these radio stations a visit on your promotional tour. We buy your music too as well as listen to it. Also I hope you are going to go back to the true Sean Paul and start making good music again. If not trust me infinitely I will be on your case. Don't like the new shit that you have out. I know you want to do something different but stay true to your roots I have ideas but them be my ideas son.

People I am raving about SWAY. I recently picked up a copy of the magazine and I can hold my head up and say I am extremely proud to be Black. Black people and whites too any how you don't support them I will be angry. I infinitely love the magazine. Sway for me can I see some more brothers as male models. I want to go yes never mind because if I continue I am go going to go overboard but please some more black male models please. Just for me.

Now back on board.

Remember everyone is looking to America and looking at the American Dollar but no one is looking at Africa and the people that live in Africa. Soon the American Dollar won't be worth the paper it is printed on because I dream time and time again their money as well as gas spiralling downwards. Hey it's a dream and so far many of the things I have seen have come to pass.

Right now everyone is in a cash grab. Raping the poor and pocketing more but none know that this is just a prelude and escalation for disaster.

Airlines are getting ridiculous with demands that have nothing to do with terror but their own pocket book but it has to be this way. Soon you will hear you cannot travel without the mark of the beast. We have the mark of the beast already. It is the Social Security Card and Social Insurance Number. Without these we can't buy a home, get a job, nor can we sell anything. Business this is your Business Number but at the rate we are going this number will become a more sinister plot to get people to concede to the will of the devil. Trust me many will die because the ultimate virus has not yet hit the global market as yet. This virus that will devour and yes it will be air bourn.

**Black People what will you do because the majority of corporations are not black or Jamaican owned. Currently Jamaica has nothing to stand on and when this new system is implemented how will you save yourself?**

**How will your children survive?**

**Do not think that God will help?**

**This time around God will truly be gone.**

**You will run to the mountain and the mountain will flee meaning the mountain will already be gone because not one of you know about the mountain.**

- *Martin Luther King told you*

- *Moses told you*

- *I am now telling you that the mountain is God himself*

- *When God select you to do his work you see the mountain and how beautiful it is.*

- *You will see the tree of life. Bob Marley called the tree the freedom tree and it is beautiful.*

- *The mountain has people on it and this is why Martin Luther King Jr. said he has been to the mountain top. He may not get there with you......and he continued on with his speech. Know the quote. Remember it because this quote is important to your history. It is important to you. Did Moses not go up to the mountain. Put the pieces together and know.*

And for you the people that will now come and use the mountain and say you have seen the mountain I caution you on this. Stop dicking around with peoples' lives because the mountain has nothing to do with Religion the MOUNTAIN IS GOD but when we see the mountain we see an actual mountain because this is how our eyes can perceive it.

- *I have seen the mountain more than once and on this mountain you find Chinese and Black at the first level. The grass is green and beautiful, everything in perfect harmony. When you go further up the mountain you find White people only and at the top you find all Blacks. This is how I saw it and this is how I am relating it to you and I will not change it to please any given race. I did not see religion no form of religion there.*

- *The only race I did not see there is the Indian and Spanish race and this is sad.*

- *ONCE AGAIN THE 3 RACES I SAW WERE:*

  BLACKS

  CHINESE

  WHITES

Jamaican's I am telling you that it is going to get worse and you have to prepare yourself because shortly all that you have you will truly have nothing. Famine and drought is going to ravish your land there is no ands ifs or buts about this. If the famine don't hit you a devastating earthquake will and it is looming. Trust me you will never recover from it

Right now your water supply is scarce

You are getting below average rainfall

There is fewer farmers on the island because the older generation are dying out and many cannot work on the farm any more

Your children are lagging behind in the education department because it seems the more educated they get the more back-a-wall they become.

We put value on status

We show off on the poor

We could not care less about our fellowman

We couldn't even care less about our children and yes now I am going to go off on the parents. **How**

the hell can you as a nation see the atrocities happening to your children and condone it. Madda –oman and yes I am going to get vulgar here. Unnu sell unnu pussy, fuck from one man to the next like leggo beast and have not a care in the world for your children. Over 1500 young kids went missing in Jamaica and the island is not talking about it. What you think you fuck and get them and that's it. Kacky sell a shop noa dat. It's called a fucking sex toy. Clean your damned act up. How the hell can you labour and feel so much pain and not look after your children. Dem no jus cum so. As parents do your damned jobs. How much Annada alert should the island have.

Black Hearts no dun inna Jamaica.

How much more of your kids must be sold into slavery? Come on now. We cry about how our people were sold into slavery so many centuries ago but yet we are the ones to sell our own out. We put the blame on other nations and we the black race is selling our own race out. ***We are selling our children.***

We are trafficking our children to the United States and no one in the international

___community is crying out.___ Everyone is tight lipped about it. People this has to stop.

People I am going to be vulgar here again.

Some a unnu parents know the truth but say unnu no noa and unnu know.

What unnu pussy neva hot unnu when di pickney a cum. Unna neva halla fi pain so how the hell can you as a mother sit back and not cry out to your government to do something.

How the hell can the United States government sit back and allow the trafficking of human beings into its country. It's not all about drugs Jamaican children are being sold into slavery in your country what the hell are you doing about it. What Jamaican kids or black children values nothing in your book. They are children just like yours. They don't have a voice because they are innocent. Who is taking up for them?

Like I've said Jamaicans we are fucking worthless. No mother in their right mind would do something so anus. I guess the saying is right in Jamaica anything goes and all we do is seek to rob, rape and kill each other.

These are children people. Do you know what is happening to them? Dear God the thought of grown ass men and woman using unnu pickney dem as sex toys.

Tell me something cocky deya factory so when one pickney gaane unnu jus gaa di factry and breed again.

Where the fuck are the fathers in all of this?

Why are you the fathers sitting down on your asses and not doing something about this?

Oh ya I forgot you are all the factories, machines that were made to service. Yes robots without emotions.

God some are working as sex slaves.

Some of them are cleaning people's house

Some of them are being murdered for their organs

Jamaica a diss unnu a sell out unnu pickney fa. Everyone a wi a sell dem out because none a wi a do nothing bout it.

Unnu love unnu politics more than unnu children

Every year unnu a kill unnu self ova politics but yet the serious issues that plagues your land does not concerns you.

Unnu radda walla in a shit than do anything to uplift yourself and your nation.

How much ANNADA alert must you have?

Over 1500 hundred children went missing. Yes some were rescued but what about the over 500 in 2011 that were not recovered.

Tell me how much more will we lose in 2012 and beyond?

Look at your island. You own nothing and you are proud. Take a damned good look at yourself and do a hell of a lot better.

You have a new government now. Don't think because you have a new Prime Minister Hell has been taken from you. It hasn't. Nothing she does or do can or will save you from your pending destruction. Your previous government made sure of this. Their final act of betrayal was Air God. They sold God and no one revolted meaning protested and said you can't do that. When you do that you are selling out God. ***We sold out God*** _**in the air and land. We betrayed God. Now the world can look at us and say yes the black nation crucified God. They were the Judas that sold him out for dirty pieces of silver and none of us can say this is a lie because Air Jamaica is not Jamaican owned but Trinidadian owned.**_

Portia you are in office now. Do right by your people and get the nation on the right track. Like I've said neither you – your party or the previous government have the economic smarts to bring Jamaica forward. Prove me wrong and step up to the plate.

Forget the old ideals and slave owner mentality. Go back to the teachings of Marcus Garvey by reading what he said about blacks becoming progressive. You cannot keep that negative mental attitude and think this is going to move Jamaica forward because it will not. Jamaica has the resources utilize it and let these resources remain in the hands of Jamaicans. Yes there are foreign policies that every nation have to adhere to but make these foreign policies work for the benefit of Jamaica and Jamaicans.

Be the first nation to squash the Buggery law because as it is Jamaica is violating people's God given rights. These people are humans and none of you as heads of state have a right to enact laws against them. These laws are illegal and demeaning and infinitely do not represent God.

Do not listen to the leaders of the church because these leaders do not have anything to do with God. They know not God nor do they work for God. They do not work on the behalf of God.

You will get opposition from them and a lot of Jamaicans but do that which is right in the sight of God and not man.

The church cannot tell people how to live in their homes because the churches do not practice the will of God. Anyone that tells you to discriminate against others is not of God. They are going against God because God is true love and he does not discriminate based on sexual preference, colour of skin, eye colour and the clothes that you wear.

When they come to you and tell you that God destroyed Sodom and Gomorrah because they were Sodomites refer them to June 1692 the sinking of Port Royal and the vile acts Jamaican's committed then. Port Royal was the new Sodom and Gomorrah. Port Royal did sink so what are they saying. Other nations have gay rights and they did not sink nor is God punishing them but Port Royal sank so truly think and repeal the Buggery Law.

Right now Jamaica is on the brink of destruction and it is not because of homosexuality it is because of the corruption, the vile murders, the adultery, the slavery, the rape and many other things that plague the country. You cannot rape people of their dignity. *Human trafficking is happening in your country, grown ass men are raping babies, your country is broke these are issues that also need to be addressed. Address them and stop with the crap of breaking away from England because you of yourself know you are not running the country. You want Jamaica to become a Republic truly think of your actions because once Jamaica becomes a Republic then I feel sorry for Jamaicans because you would not be able to stop the drug cartels from taking over the island. Both political parties are funded by these cartels and some of them are in the house of parliament down there. Jamaica isn't run by the government but by these cartels because many of you are eating out of their pots. I need not have to go further than Dudus. I know if things do not change and Jamaica become a Republic the country will become like Mexico and other parts of South America and you know this. More innocent people will lose their lives.* Did you even think about the returnee's that collect pension for the UK and other countries? What about the impact on them and how would they be able to collect their money? You have to think and the people around you have to think. We all want money but do it the legal way – the honest way. Whether you or your key officials and these drug cartels like it or not they won't survive the economic crisis that is to come because everyone will feel the pinch. Like I've said Jamaica is struggling and smuggling and we need to take care not just for the rich but also for the poor.

Also know this it is a known fact that animals of the same sex sleep with each other. There is no difference when it comes to humans. What are we going to say animals have no sense?

I have told the Rastas about the genes. None of us know the true meaning of the genes.

Look at the female genes XX meaning that they are the same - Homo and XY meaning Hetro. As it is for humans it is for animals. Like I said the truth lies within your genes ***and Jamaicans don't go be bashing women with your ignorant self and say women are the cause of this. Know the full truth and not some watered down crap that people give you to soak up.***

Yes you can condemn me and be up in arms but at the end of the day the truth must be know before destruction comes.

You cannot deny people their God given right.

God does not do it to you so why do it to others?

There are things that you cannot comprehend and if God is teaching you learn. And for all of you that say I am a Lesbian you can all kiss my ass.

Some of you go to church and commit so much vile acts it's amazing. After you have done it you go around and say you are a child of God. The clergy do more to mock and defile God than anyone else on the face of this planet.

No you don't. Let's put it this way Moses Moses take off thy shoes because the place you are standing on is holy ground. Remember I told you

**above that the Ethiopians did this to God and you are following them. You are doing the same thing to God as the Ethiopians did. Then you turn around and mock God by singing this song.**

Now tell me who is hell bound and who does God hate? I know God does not but I use hate for a lack of a better word. It is the only word I can use to describe how God truly feels.

None of you can say you are not mocking and condemning God. By going to church does not make you a child of God it just makes you in league with Satan. You become the children of Satan and trust me you all are.

Portia do right by your people you don't have to listen to me but Jamaica and your constitution cannot continue to violate the rights of its people. This is wrong and you know it.

We are all human beings and if you truly love God and live for God no one can get you out of office no matter how hard they try. God will protect you but you have to be clean. Do things that are truthful and right in the eyes of God.

You have the power to put Jamaica on the right track do so honestly. Do not sell anymore of

Jamaica out. Come on now. Let the slackness stop. Let every member of your cabinet be accountable for their wrongs. I am going to say this and please do not it the wrong way and I am not way saying that you are dirty. Answer me this if the head is dirty how can the body be clean?

God got rid of the dirt and made you the head do right by God. And don't think I won't see what you are doing because I will see and trust me I will tell so know how you walk. If you walk dirty I will see it and many others will too. Jamaica need a wakeup call. Young children cannot continue to go missing and nothing is being done about it. ***Slavery was abolished long ago so why is Jamaica continuing with the practice.*** I don't know if you have children but as a mother, a woman, a human being you have to do something. Hold everyone accountable, the police, the citizens of Jamaica and we that are overseas condoning and engaging in this practice.

The police cannot sweep things under the rug because they fear retaliation from people high up. They have children too. How would they feel if it was their child being taken? Come on now.

We let people think bad of us and some of us hold our heads down in shame because of what is happening out there. We have to do better not just for ourselves but also for the betterment of our country. We say we run things things no run wi but guess what things a run wi because each and every day we turn a blind eye to what's happening down there (in Jamaica).

Yes some of the people greedy and licky licky but that is the choice that they made

We can no longer sell out our country out to the highest bidder and think this is good for the people on a whole.

What about the future of Jamaicans?

What about the future of our children and grand children?

What about them? Think

None of you are also taking into consideration Global Warming

It will affect Jamaica as well

More hurricanes and earthquakes in the form of Tsunami's will happen

Islands will sift from their present location and some will be lost meaning sink

Do not say it cannot happen because it will

This is what took place billions of years ago but that Tsunami caused the earth to shift out of alignment with the other planets and yes caused nations to shift from its original location

And scientists do not say this cannot happen because you've proven this with Japan shifting 17 miles from its exact location with the recent Tsunami that they had

Rich people many of you think you won't be left poverty stricken but trust me you will.

Many of you will be left penniless because whether you like it or not disastrous change is coming and this we can blame on ourselves.

There will be a global economic meltdown if we do not change the way we do business.

Everything is based on greed and it is greed that will take you all down.

Revelations told you about Wormwood. ***So people do not go on a panic attack because I know many*** *of you will. Do not sell your possessions either. That will be just dumb on your part. Many of us see things but cannot explain it. I've told you I've seen a green and gold moon in the Northeast of Canada. I do not know what it means. Maybe someone out there knows. Not everything that we get we can interpret and if you read Daniel it told you this. This is why I say do not panic.*

Now Jamaican's with all this said, you know of wormwood, when this comet gets here tell me something who will be left on the planet?

Say we survive this comet

What about radiation, diseases

Purity of water

Many of us will be left without electricity because you are on the electrical grid

How will be able to communicate because many of us depend on satellites to send information wirelessly

If the satellites are down and they will come crashing down how are you going to watch television, hear the news?

Some are saying fibre optics

The Radio

Lava rising that's all I got to say when it comes to fibre optics

Not going to happen some of you are saying

Think about the heat because the temperature on earth right now is unstable. In some parts of the world winter has turned into spring and in many countries water is scarce. Dormant volcanoes are erupting. Trust me lava will be spuing soon.

It took us 100 years to get where we are.

How much longer will it take us to clean ourselves and this planet up?

Jamaica and Jamaican's alike you are no exception to what is to come

You cannot adopt the principles of the Babylonians

You cannot live for greed

Help each other and stop cutting the next man down.

Why should you be the only one to eat bread and the other man go hungry?

I retract that because JAMAICA YOU OWN NOTHING SO YOU WILL GO HUNGRY

Many of you will become beggars in the streets because you made it so

Now-a-days you tell your child to farm he looks at you funny and say im naa farm im han too clean fi farm

Tell me how the hell do you expect to eat in the next 2-5 years if that?

Look at your unemployment rate. It's not getting any better so you better pick up the gardening tools and plant your tomato, callaloo and yam

Kids make mango juice at mango time and sell it

There are so many things you can do to help yourself

Scout of the place and see what sells, talk to your parents and see if they can help you but do something for you. Don't become a beggar because guess what many of those rich Jamaican's that look down upon you will be the ones that will come to you and beg from you. They will come to you for something to eat and drink if they don't smarten up

Remember old time granny sey the higher the monkey climb the more im expose

Dem did tell wi sey what goes up must come down

Everyone a follow the market trend and none realize that a greater depression looms and many will lose it all because the stock market will come crashing down.

All of you that are hiding your money in foundations trust me they too will come crashing down also

Everything will collapse because greed and evil made it so

Youth man truss mi so listen to Cujo, he's a Canadian Reggae Singer that sing Youth Man Be Careful. Listen to the song and truly be careful.

No falla company because when you are doing for self bad mine meaning your jealous friends will call you idiat and tell you crap to make you fail. Don't listen to them because when you have your money dem a di same one wey a cum look fi hand out from you. Dem no memba how dem shot you down.

Dem no memba how you encourage them.

Help you.

If you have good grades and love to teach tutor and *YOU THE TEACHERS DO NOT GO INTO THE MARKET DAMN GREEDY. LET THE KIDS MAKE THE MONEY. THE GOVERNMENT ALREADY PAYS YOU.*

I DON'T CARE HOW SMALL IT IS LET THE YOUTHS EAT FOOD AND STAY THE HELL OUT OF THE TUTORING BUSINESS.

AS FOR YOU MR. PERVERT KEEP YOUR DAMNED PENIS IN YOUR PANTS. THIS DOES NOT GIVE YOU ACCESS TO MOLEST PEOPLE'S CHILDREN. SO CHILDREN THINK IF YOU CAN TUTOR AT SCHOOL IN THE EVENINGS OR AT THE LIBRARY DO SO.

THINK OF YOUR SAFETY AND PARENTS MONITOR YOUR CHILDREN BECAUSE I KNOW HOW CUNNING SOME OF THESE STUDENTS ARE. AND NO I WILL NOT

REMIND YOU. YOU ARE PARENT SHOULD KNOW.

Jamaican writers and television producers expand your horizon in Africa.

Set up more theatrical and dance companies. Jamaica we can dance and act let's give Canada and America, the world a run for their money. Get into the market of making world class movies. I want to see some of you at TIFF – Toronto International Film Festival.

Develop the country and attract Movie companies to your country therefore bringing money into the country and please protect the trees because we need it. Trust me we are so going to need it at the rate the earth's climate change is going.

Plant more trees and protect that which you have because trust me Jamaica is going to get hotter and water is going to become more scarce. We had better start replanting those cactus trees that we so blatantly destroyed.

Protect your rivers and stop dumping human and animal waste in it because you will need the water. It is a part of your drinking supply so protect it and do not flush your outdoor toilets in it. Some of you are plain out nasty.

Jamaican's like I've said we are innovative and inventive so come up with ways to use the sea water for human consumption because we know how low the water supply gets. Mi caane spell it out for you. Lade God find a way to extract the salt out of di sea wata no man and mek it drinkable. Yes mi noa sey mi crazy but mi mine a run wey wit mi.

Listen, better yet hey Mr. Billionaire Jamaican, how about setting up a recycling depot in Jamaica so that the surrounding Caribbean Islands can use it and charge them a fee per metric tonne or whatever.

How about incineration as well that could work

Black People we have to think we can't just sell ourselves short we have to start owning some of these multinational companies as well.

We have to be relevant and future ready or we will be left in the cold. We can't just stay stuck in North America. We have to help our country then expand to the motherland and help her.

This was what Marcus Garvey was trying to educate you on. We are not limited to the environment we live in. Stop trying to build someone else's country meaning if you are failing in North America look to the Caribbean and Africa. I know it will not be easy but it is a start.

We cannot give up our home no matter what. Some of our forefathers came from Africa as slaves. Many died on the way and none has yet to make an apology and we do not need it because hell is there for those slave owners we know this.

- We are living and we cannot forget where we came from.

- We cannot let other nations tell us where we came from when we know that we created this universe

- We cannot forget nor should we forget because slavery will happen again if we do not wake up and stop selling each other out

- Black people we are the worst for disunity

- We don't want nor like to see our own rise to the top and that is sad

- We can no longer be house slaves

- We have to learn to respect each other

- Yes some people reach the top by doing wrongs but it is them and not you

Know that we are perfect the way we are and no matter what we are all, no we are not all God's people because some of us have sold our souls to the devil so I will retract that statement.

Listen all I am saying is that God does not hate based on race and yes I will sound racist and you are entitled to call me racist that is your given right. It's just the way I write and if you are white and reading this book I have to get through to my people.

Trust me you are no exception to the rule I will call you wukliss so if you are White Jamaican, Chinese Jamaican, Black or Indian Jamaican you are under the same banner and all of you wukliss.

Unnu a bane ya and in my book there is so no distinction unnu wukliss.

No I do not see colour, race or creed when I am talking to you the Jamaican race. All I see is Jamaican and unnu wukliss.

When I write there is no White Jamaican here. You stand under the banner honey so take your punishment like a true Jamaican.

Yes cuss mi noa di BC's dem to. Like I said anno spit doa.

So when it comes to Jamaica's economic crisis do not take yourself out of the picture and remember the motto OUT OF MANY ONE PEOPLE.

Jamaica is your home and none a wi can say come out. Come out wey. You too have to stand up and do your part and stop raping the island because you were born under the banner and all of you know how blessed Jamaica is so forget your petty little trash talk and help your country. Be proud of it because Jamaica is not for blacks alone it is for you too.

Don't even say you wouldn't figure that from the way I write.

Now I can tell the lot of you to kiss my ass. I told you above when I write about Jamaica and Jamaican's I do not see colour or class. I refuse to. Jamaica is for Jamaican's so if you think otherwise that is your damned problem and you can more than doublely kiss my ass.

Do not ask me how to explain it. I can't because to me you are all black anyway.

Any of you say otherwise I will repeat KISS MY ASS. This is just me. Once you know more about spirituality you will comprehend this. It's weird I know but some things in life are weird.

So Jamaica as I close this book what will your choice be?

You have risen from the depths of slavery

Plucked from the motherland

You have been used and abused

Robbed of your pride and dignity

Now the plot thickens

The sand in the hourglass runs low

The ship sinks

Economic divide

Uncertain future

Chaos and confusion looms

Greed has taken form

The innocent cry

Death walks in your land

Starvation comes

The young population refuse to farm

They lay in wait at curb sides

Waiting to lure their next victim

Economic restraint none

People living in ignorance

Still waiting the return of their saviour while their children go hungry-unfed

The sign of the times is now a reality

No one wants to change

Blood will run

Many send their children, mothers and fathers to an early grave

Yes everyone refuse to listen

Climate changes

Economic downfall

Depression

Suicide on the increase

Another Black Empire fall

Yes gone to the dogs

All will be forgotten

Another race gone from the history books because they would not listen

We gave the devil the upper hand

We opened the door for him

He came

Took all he wanted

Left another country in utter disrepair

Ruin

Africa we want to come home we cry

God you have forsaken us you will cry

But none remember the words of the RASTA MAN

Heritage gone

Faceless

Nameless

Out of Many we've become None.

Tell me Jamaica who will protect you from your eventual downfall?

To the youths of Jamaica I dedicate Youth Man by Cujo and Same Gun by QQ to all of you because whether you like it or not you are the future of Jamaica and you need to wake up.

It makes no sense to pick up the gun. I know a lot of you are saying if father was around things would be better but you don't have a father. You have your mother that is raising you. Some of you grandparents are raising you. ***Mama and grandparents are sending you to school go to school. You have the important parent raising*** *you so be thankful. No matta if fada and mada no dey, no matta mi youth love the one that is raising you, feeding you and clothing you.*

Listen to good teaching and do something positive with your life.

It's a hard road to walk and many times not enough food is there

Mama can't find a dollar to buy food

You see the hardness of life on her face as well as your face but don't give up because my children was once there.

Just to let you in on a part of my life. Many times I want to give up on them and have said I give up on them and want to run away and here I am doing what I truly love.

Don't let the ones that truly love you and doing their best to feed and clothe you hold their head down in shame

And by no means think I still have it easy because I don't.

I've cried too and ask why me but those why me's are my lessons learnt, lessons I teach my children,

I tell them to get their education because it is vital in life. I tell them to choose positive women

Women that know what they want out of life

Women that are clean, respectful and progressive and I am now telling you this as a mother. No matter what I write and what your parents think of me. Hold your head up. Never hold it down because in life we grow, we grow up not down.
Look at you you are getting older not younger. You are no longer a baby. With each year that goes by learn from it. Let it be your life lesson and teach your children wisely.

Always be there for them no matter what and don't think that some woman will not make your life hell.

Some will so know the woman you marry, the woman you pick up. Before you pick a woman pray to God and tell God the qualities you want in a woman. Loving, caring, progressive and clean.

Ask God to give you these qualities in your children before you have them. As God to make them obedient and never walk on the way of evil.

Bug God and wait on him because it does take time and yes I told my children these things as these things my mother never taught me so now I am teaching you as a mother and a woman that truly care and love you.

Mama will cuss yu, granny will cuss yu, mi cuss fi mi pickney dem to. Mi cuss Jamaica and the people to not because I hate them but because I truly love them and want to see them do better. I want to live to see Jamaica up there with developed nations when it comes to world class everything.

Jamaica no noa how much mi love di Island.

Truss mi if I had the money like the richest man in the world Jamaica debt would be paid off but since I do not have it I have to cuss unnu fi unnu fi wake up and do better.

Listen even if you don't have a job no one can fool you because you can read and you are the one that read the fine prints and find the hidden glitches contained in a contract. You are the one to read granny letter word for word and tell her.

Be proud of you and remember NOT ALL MOTHER'S ARE MOTHER'S AND NOT ALL FATHER'S ARE FATHER'S BECAUSE WHEN YOU COME TO SOMETHING THE ONES THAT WERE NOT THERE FOR YOU ARE THE ONES TO POSE YOU UP. If Mama and Daddy was never there for you never forget it but change the cycle be there for your children when you have kids.

If granny a raise yu big up granny because she is the one to suffer with you.

If mama a raise yu big up mama because she bust her ass off to send you to school.

For the single father's that are doing it alone big up yourself because you are feeling the pain and I cannot exclude you.

Youth man the road in life has a lot of pitfalls and we do fall down but you can't give up. You have to persevere and trust me you will make it.

I don't care if you want to be a Farmer

I don't care if you want to be a Vet

I don't care if you want to be a Dancer as long as you truly love the field you choose and you can see yourself doing this job for the rest of your life.

Truly love you and what you do and never ever hurt anyone in the process because it is life for life meaning if you hurt someone in the physical and get away with it you will never get away in the spiritual.

Trust me you will feel it worse in the spiritual so live your life clean and honest. Forget about the next man. Do you. Be the best person you can be.

No matta if yu no ave no shoes. If you only have one pair of shoes take care of it and make it last until you can afford to get another one. Meaning mommy or granny can buy you another pair.

If any of you ever want to talk hit me up while I am in Jamaica. Stop and talk to me. Question me on things and if I can't give you an answer I will direct you on where to find it.

Note of Caution I make look intimidating but I am not. I like to talk when I am down there. There's a freedom in the air down there it's like you can accomplish anything. That nice vibe in the air you breathe. It's so hard to explain.

Jamaican's if you are not a part of the solution then you are a part of the problem. When I look at the state of Jamaica's economy I can safely say that we are all meaning all Jamaican's whether living at home or abroad are all a part of the problem.

As stated above none of us can say we truly love Jamaica and watch it crumble like this. Infinitely trust me on this something is going to happen to Jamaica and soon. I cannot remember my dream when I was down there but I know something is going to happen to the country. Dear God if it disaster all of us can kiss Jamaica goodbye.

Gunman you can target me for the statement I made above but truth is you are also apart of Jamaica's problem. Every Jamaican on the island and abroad is a part of Jamaica's problem because we all know that Jamaica is a blessed island and all of us want to see it sink-be destroyed.

We cannot go on this way. No race, colour or creed on the island is excluded. You are Jamaican. You were born there and all of you are reaping the blessings of the island.

How can we say Jamaica is blessed and we are proud to be Jamaican's when Jamaican's owns nothing on the island? We let people come in and buy out the island. Tell me Jamaica what is truly left for Jamaican's as a whole?

To sum up everyone need to look back truly look back at ourselves and see where we are heading.

The downfall of Jamaica

+ *No Bauxite*
+ *No Air God meaning Air Jamaica and yes I am still bent anna screw because we sold God to the Trinity-WE MEANING ALL JAMAICAN'S SOLD OUT AIR JAMAICA AND I DON'T CARE WHAT PART OF THE GLOBE YOU ARE IN WE SOLD OUT GOD. I REPEAT WE SOLD GOD OUT FOR THIRTY PIECES OF SILVER. NO PROPERLY PUT FOR DIRTY PIECES OF SILVER. WE CRUCIFIED GOD BECAUSE WE NO LONGER HAVE AIR GOD OR GOD AIR. Come on now. We sold God out and we are proud of this. Truss mi and I refuse to hide my conscience if a Caribbean Airline fi get fi mi money. Money woulda stap mek. Mi radda walk to Jamaica than fly. Mi fi mi sweet sweet Jamaica. Keep Caribbean Airlines. All when unnu change back di name to Air Jamaica mi naa fly with unnu because sey ano Jamaican Owned.*

- *Jamaica has no viable manufactured goods to export. This you can blast me on because I know we export yams and so forth*
- *Poor education system*
- *Poor housing*
- *Lack of progressive people*
- *Corrupt politicians*
- *Corrupt people*
- *Corrupt everything*
- *Poor roads*
- *Country bankrupt*
- *Failed as well as lack of adequate government policies*
- *Escalated crime – violence*
- *Lack of tourism*
- *Substandard health care system*
- *No long term policies*
- *Policies that are geared to the elite without taking into consideration the poor*
- *Land eroding*
- *Standard of living way below the poverty line*
- *Failing judicial system*
- *Outdated laws*
- *Outdated hospitals and schools*
- *No economic growth because you still import more than you export*
- *Failing no crumbling economic structure*
- *Economically the country is dead – bankrupt*

+ *No positive economic strategies to move forward in the global marketplace*
+ *In a nutshell the country right now as of 2011 - dead*

All of these we have to look at because Jamaica is governed by greed and more greed. Drug lords owning politicians telling them what to do and how to govern the country and this cannot be.

Drug lords I am talking to you now. You own the politicians and some of you are politicians and yes you can hate me and mark me for death but truth is you are a part of Jamaica's problem and this must stop.

I don't care how you make your money, I don't care about who you kill from who you don't kill I care and infinitely care about Jamaica and if you are not going to be a part of the solution in maintaining and fixing Jamaica then get the fuck off the island. You are corrupting a blessed island so stop the bullshit. Let your money help the country now. Do something positive for Jamaica instead of letting people think that we are hogs and pigs, murderer's and beggars.

The land is eroding all across the island, roads need to be fixed, some roads have craters upon craters in it and you have the money invest some in the island. Come on now. You cannot pocket the wealth for yourself. Shit think man. Jamaica is broke. The island is in utter disrepair and you see it, know it and doing nothing about it. You cannot let the country sink. This global depression will affect you also.

You will have nothing when this great depression comes.

You have your money locked away in another country.

All I got to say is Global depression not recession depression.

Tell me something was Port Royal not enough?

It sank to the bottom of the sea and at the rate Jamaica is going this time around it will be the entire island to sink.

Once it sinks no one will be around to tell the tales because you will go down in history as a nation of people that do not listen, a nation of people that live for corruption, live to beg, live to kill.

Mu and Atlantis sank and you Jamaica is next because the bell does toll for you and like I said and will forever say I want and need something really bad to happen to the island for the lot of you to wake up but in hindsight that won't help because no matter the hurricane's and your recent earthquake you are still go on in your corrupt ways.

The vileness will continue because the lot of you will be saying I can do what I want.

Some of you are saying I am crazy and no one will listen to you because you don't know what you are talking about.
You would have become like the Children of Noah.

Continue on like I said fiya daa muss muss tail im tink a cool breeze.

Watch and see if Jamaica no wipe off the face of the planet if unnu continue with unnu dutty ways.

Mi no affi sey nothing because if what I saw and can't remember was destruction then woe be unto you.

Like I've said you can mark me for death, try to kill me it is your prerogative. All of you need to think about the future of your children and grandchildren and stop living in ignorance.

Every one of us need to open our eyes and listen to what Marcus Garvey said. We need to have enterprise, we need to think progressive and stop with the regressive mentality. Jamaican's have money, the government and country does not. We need to stop:

- *Selling ourselves short*
- *Stop raping the country*
- *Stop killing ourselves*
- *We need to preserve Jamaica for Jamaican's so that when other's see us they can say we are truly blessed and highly favoured by God*
- *We cannot continue to sell the country out*
- *We cannot keep turning a blind eye to the immediate problems that face us*
- *For example, the roads across the island are in deplorable conditions and nothing is truly being done to fix them. How can we say we want tourist to enjoy the beauties of Jamaica when we do not have adequate roads to accommodate them.*

How can we say we need young people or more young people to run the country when young and old are not suitable to run Jamaica?

Meaning we are not progressive in thought. None is capable of catapulting Jamaica in a positive and economic way.

None is capable of catapulting Jamaica economically in the twenty first and twenty second century. Well that's if mankind live that long.

Jamaica cannot continue on the backwards course it is on. We need to stop thinking backwards well eloquently put by Mr. Marcus Mosiah Garvey we cannot think regressive we have to think progressive.

Jamaican people we can no longer let politician's dictate our lives for us meaning when politics time come around they give you a thousand dollars and some food to buy your votes and as soon as that person is elected he does nothing to help the community. When you go to him or her for help you are told a buy dem buy yu vote. Come on that is crap.

Jamaica I am reeling now because I see so many things that is not right happening in the same old Jamaica and nothing is being done about it. Not because some of you are poor well a lot of you but you have a voice.

You know I truly love and cherish Jamaica because when I come out there I see the beauty in the landscape, the mountainous terrain and I am awed, awe struck by it and I say to myself why can't you see what I see. Some of you need to get up and truly look at the green green grass of home.

Truly love your country and try to help it not carry it down.

Jamaica you have free medicare do not lose it. Come on now.

Rich and middle class stop raping the system.

Free medicare was meant for the poor let them utilize it. You of yourself can pay for private doctors and your medicine so do it. Come on now man have a damn conscience.

When you rape the system what about the poor?

Jamaica is not for you alone so stop because one day God will turn the tides on you and you never know when you will become a pauper. If there is no medicare you will die.

Now once again all of you Jamaican's that can afford medicare meaning you are paying these private medical insurance companies utilize that policy or coverage. You're paying them so stop sinking Jamaica further into economic debt. It's amazing how all of you say yes man mi a Jamaican, mi love mi country but yet kill the country, sink it further into economic turmoil and debt.

It would be a shame to see the government cancel free medicare for the poor because they can no longer afford it.

Think American's have been fighting for this and you have it but many rape the system. Stop it man come on now. You have the money spend it because when you are dead you cannot spend it. Help Jamaica cunyo.

Back to you Mr. Bad Man. Help Jamaica you have the money spend some of it on the roads so that tourist can explore the island and spend some of their money.

We need to attract more tourists to come and spend money on the island so the country can pay its bills. Curve the violence now man come on. Yu no love Jam Dung come on man. Think. Jamaica is broke. Tourism that the island depend on is lagging and you are helping to sink the country.

Tell mi something your pickney dem no let me put it in English. Your children reside on the island, some go to school there as well as abroad. When more economic hard times hit Jamaica and the GCT hit dollar for dollar meaning for every dollar you spend you have to pay a dollar for GCT what then?

Jamaica's GCT is at 40% right now and rising what then?

If it continues to rise as a matter of fact I can so see the GCT hitting 100% given the current economic trend of Jamaica. I won't even have to tell you what will happen on the island because as Bob Marley said many more will have to suffer and many more will have to die. If you don't believe me that's good because now you know and knowledge is the key.

Like Marcus Garvey said if we don't know where we are from how do we know where we are going?

We cannot live like the blind nor can we continue to live like the lost.

We are not lost. We know who we are and where we are from so let's start living instead of dying.

Don't take my word for it listen to Bob Marley

Listen to Truth Is by Duane Stephenson

Listen to Save the World by Peetah Morgan.

You have your future in your hand so use this time the little time you have left wisely.

There are many things Jamaica can do to come out of its current economic slump but we need to change our mind set and get off the regressive mode and onto the progressive mode.

I am going to repeat myself we need to change our way of thinking from regressive to progressive.

Some of the solutions mentioned above if they can work let it work for Jamaica and do not sell them out. Keep them in Jamaica.

Tourists there are many stores in the Kingston airport and I am glad to see the food court so my prior book has so become redundant. Meaningless now.

Save a twenty or forty dollars and spend it in the duty free shops. I didn't get a chance to explore the prices, nor the facility in-depth but buy the food and drinks especially the natural made juices. Enjoy yourself in the duty free lounge because you don't know when you'll be coming back to Jamaica and trust me the next time I go back I will be going buck wild because I saw some things that I want to buy if not explore. Trust me love Jamaica mad mad mad.

Jamaica if my books start to sell Bull Head Mountain the road will be my task, my project because I aim on fixing the road straight to the top. I want to go camping up there. Bull Head love you. Naturist, tourist no trip is complete without going to the top of Bull Head Mountain. It is gorgeous and serene for me. Blessed.

Jamaica plant more trees up there. Coconut, Mango and keep it natural and nun a unno Jamaican betta pollute it an sey unnu a go put shop up dey or house up dey. Not a rass. Keep it natural because I want to sleep under the stars up there as nature intended it.

Now Mr. Jamaican man that has money let your mind roll now. Think. There is a town not too far from the mountain build a bread and breakfast in the square and give tours. If you don't want to give tours let the taxi man dem do it. Let them make a bread and missa taxi man don't rob the people them because you are making money.

Think. Be glad now because more money a come in. And Jamaica do not charge a fee to go up the mountain. Hire a park ranger and people to keep the mountain clean. What you can do if people want to plant a coconut tree or a mango tree let them buy the sucker from an accredited store that is located in the square. You the Jamaican government can run this establishment. I know not everyone is going to want to plant trees but you must keep Bull Head Natural. Tourist, naturist keep my mountain clean. Yes it's my mountain because I love it. Don't piss me off because I am very hot headed. Blue Mountain I am going to explore you don't worry.

Hey Mr. Tourist if that's not your cup of tea. Milk River Spa is it. The area is old and it may not be your cup of tea but check it out. The water is nice and guess what get that massage to get the kinks out of your body. Stay overnight at the hotel and enjoy. Don't just sit in the resort areas explore the island. Jamaica is beautiful. You can't spend your money in the tourist areas all the time. Get out and see Jamaica. There's a craft market in Ochi Rios explore it. You may not buy anything but explore the market. I love going to May Pen Market. It's congested and I love it just seeing the people sell in the sun. I don't know I just love Jamaican Markets so big up to all the people that sell in May Pen Market, Spanish Town, Old Harbour nuff respect.

Also nuff respect to the young youth's that are trying to make a dollar. I commend you for being out in the sun all day hussling. Many of you are selling phone cards, jelly coconut, mango, guinep, *you name it. Never give up keep on trodding so people home comers buy something from the youth dem. If you don't need anything that's alright but take full advantage of the coconut because the jelly and water is good for your heart as well as your high blood pressure.*

Jamaica bless and blessed all the time. Never forget your roots and stop saying you will never go back to Jamaica. Hotel dey you zimmi. You don't have to stay with family. Spend it at a hotel and when you are coming back duty free, duty free, duty free get mi.

Yeah, yeah the money you are saying. Well start saving from now and when you are out there get a nice sea bath. Don't leave the island without going to the sea and yes there are public beaches in Discovery Bay. Utilize it and take full advantage of the food. Yes you have to pay for the food. Buy a food for me and eat it. If you don't want food buy a ice cream cone or a juice and enjoy it for me. Come on people life is too short not to enjoy it.

Mr. Bad Man mi dey pon unnu case eee man. You si di coconut trash wey wi dash wey can we mulch it and make something with the mulch? Find out how we can turn the coconut trash into something.

Jamaica you grow so much things can we not piggy back off the Chinese economy meaning China grows a lot of tropical produce can't we sell them some of our produce, like the coconut, oranges, mangoes, sorrel, jackfruit, pomegranate so that our produce get into the international market. Do you see where I am going with this and if it cannot be done encourage tourists to try the produce because we all know there are many items such as pomegranate that is good for our health.

As for us Jamaican's that have left Jamaica many of you have your licence in HVAC. Heating and Air Conditioning. How about setting up shop in Jamaica and capitalize on this market. Come on now. You have the knowledge and skills and there are no companies that I am aware of that has shops set up in Jamaica Heating and Air Conditioning. Meaning the majority of the house do not have a water heater or central air conditioning.

Why not get in on the ground floor and take advantage of this market. Once you have the market expand to Africa like I said.

For Solar Panels and Wind Technology we may only have installers but what about technicians that can repair them when they break down .

Start networking with people you know that can repair these panels and set up shop.

As for the major corporations that reside on the island do something to maintain the island and not just rob it of its riches.

Your vehicles have to drive on the deplorable roads invest in the roads.

What are you telling me all you want is to make money off the backs of Jamaican's but refuse to invest in its infrastructure.

Help maintain the country or for a surety I will not buy your products and will tell people to boycott them. I need not call names because all of you know who you are.

Hotels the same goes for you. Hospital's are inadequately funded and equipped do your part to buy a piece of equipment here and there or buy books or computers and donate it to schools. You are making the money help the country. If you don't think this is for you.

You are all multinational owned donate a fifty or a hundred thousand if you can afford a million donate a million US no no not donate send it to the IMF or World Bank on the behalf of Jamaica debt repayment plan and pay down some of the

18.2 billion US debt. Do that much for the island because you are making money off the island.

Jamaican's abroad you do the same as well even if it's $5.00 you can send do it. Do not send the money directly to the Jamaican Government send it directly to the IMF or World Bank. We too can do our part in insuring Jamaica's future.

And stop saying you did not put Jamaica in debt. We all did. Many of us were born there and despite the pain we feel and has felt we still have to care because it is the Godly thing to do.

Many of us can go back and help even it's for just for two weeks to donate our time. Forget about the red tape take the time to become familiar and knowledgeable about Jamaica in regards to what you can do and what you cannot do.

Jamaica a fi wi and no matter it's regression we all have an opportunity to make a positive impact on the growth of the country. A lot of us are educated a broad like me take some of this knowledge back and don't think it will be easy because many Jamaican's baka wall. Meaning they are set in their ways and refuse to change.

It's as if they want to stay in their regressive ways. For all of you white Jamaican's that look down on the blacks forget it because you are oh so not white you are black. The lot of you can kiss my ass help the country because you are so not better than anyone. REMEMBER THE MOTTO "OUT OF MANY ONE PEOPLE" so you are a part of us. You were born in Jamaica I can't tell you to come out so be damned proud of your country and do all you can to make it future ready. Help the country to pay down its debt load because Mister White, Mister Syrian don't live here. Only Jamaican's live here so truly love the country and the people because whether you like it or not it is your own.

You love your wife and kids even your sweetheart. Some of unnu treat unnu sweetheart better than unnu wife so hear mi treat Jamaica better than unnu sweetheart because sey when sweetheart and wife caane feed unnu Jamaica feed unnu. Meaning you go to the back of the house and pick a mango, cut a root of cane, pick a couple oranges nyam unnu belly full and belch if not fart. So treat my sweet sweet Jamaica like the queen and king she is. Bless har up because she has been good to you.

Ah yes the churches that are collecting billions if not trillions of dollars charge them taxes on monies collected. Let the churches claim income tax.Charge taxes on tides and offerings. I told America to do this and I am telling you to do it.

It does not make any sense to lose out on billions of dollars in tax revenue because the church say so. Mister government official if you think the churches have anything to do with God read Revelations for yourself and see what it tells you about the churches and God.

I will forever repeat this "if the head is dirty the body cannot be clean" and no matter how the church justifies themselves they are not of God and will never be of God because their actions say otherwise.

Look at it this way all that is being sent up to God is dirty and filthy prayers and God is so not listening. Tell me something a preacher dey pon pulpit a preach anna sawka sawka sister Pearline an im ave im wife a yaade. Please that is so not of God.

You say you are a Christian and you are in the house of God but yet as Sunday morning come unna a sprinkle oil a tun dong, oil a kip back, oil a kill dem, oil a get post in church, oil a tan up, oil a dis and oil a dat before unnu go to church. Tell me how is this of God?

Some a unnu caane wait till payday come unnu gaane a obeah man. No mi naa joke fi real. Obeah man have a right fin nyam unnu money. Damn fool. So mister government official charge the churches taxes because no church on the face of this planet can say they were ordained by God because God never gave us dirty churches to worship in.

All of you can come with the bible and say yes the bible is real and is the truth it is from God.

Did God write it?

Many of you are saying it is divinely inspired and it's the truth I am the devil. All I got to say is I know my history, where I am coming from do you?

And I will quote again from Marcus Mosiah Garvey "if you don't know where you are coming from how do you know where you are going?"

Many of you don't know the same bible is a watered down version of black history. Many of you don't know the bible was written to keep blacks ignorant and constantly fighting for a dead man a dead God.

Many of you black people say they hate whites and some of us blacks are white oriented. Well guess what we don't bow down to a white nor a black Jesus we give thanks and praise to the true and living God. A God that is not dead but alive.

Many of you know and some don't know that King James commissioned the bible to be written and guess what King James was white. The scholars that wrote the bible are orthodox Jews and they are white so any which way you black haters look at it you are reading a white man's bible based on watered down crap. Meaning watered down and false teachings of black history so bite that because the race you so hate is the race that is teaching you and you have to bow down to their teachings because many of you bow down to a White Jesus as well as have a White Jesus in your home. So once again bite me. Sorry people but I had to get that in there somehow because I know the churches will be up in arms in regards to paying taxes.

Hey the free ride off God's back is over.

It's either these preachers step up or get the hell off God's coat tails because they are so not needed. Every Sunday you go to church and all they can do is preach from the book of the dead.

Shit give people life, teach them about life. Meaning teach people about God, how to maintain and keep God not kill God. Come on now people if you love God truly love God show him prove to him you care and you can start by cleaning up Jamaica the land of God – Ja. You have God's name so represent and live in God's

integrity. Like I've said you cannot say you love Ja-Mai-Ca and turn around and kill God. Come on now. How does that make sense? Read it and know it. Ja – God
Mai – Made
Ca – Me

Currently Jamaica import more than it export and this cannot happen. We will forever be in debt. Look at the resources around you and do something. You have ministers that are assigned posts let them do their damned job. Try to drum up more business from other nations.

POM how about using organic Jamaican Pomegranate in your juice. Have a line of Jamaican Pomegranate juices. Come on take the challenge. Let's see if Jamaican Pomegranate can give American Pomegranate a run for its money.

Grace Kennedy you sell coconut water in a can I hope some of those coconuts are Jamaican coconuts. I do drink your coconut water. I find it refreshing and great tasting. Don't like your crappy new cans though. I want the original can back. You had a good thing going and you changed it. Now I don't buy your water anymore.

Just pass yu new can dem an buy something else.

Yes another brand of coconut water. Yes they are crap but I am boycotting your coconut water because of the new crappy cans. I don't care if they are limited edition I don't like them. Stick with tradition it works for me.

Returnee's when you return home you have to try June Plum juice. It's awesome. People try the natural juices. Jamaica export, export, export June Plum Juice.

Young people you are the future of Jamaica and you need to break away from your parent's regressive mentality and start thinking progressive. Do not disrespect your parents. I repeat do not disrespect your parents but start investing in your future. Start investing in retirement saving bonds, government saving bonds, education saving bonds. Always remember tomorrow is a given and if it does not come for you it will come for your children and great grandchildren so prepare for them as well as you.

Jamaica you can cuss me, dash dutty wata pon mi but mi still a go mash unnu because I so want and need what is best for Ja- Mai-Ca the land where God made me. Live up and live, walk and live and more importantly walk before death.

Michelle

P.S. My Peeps and True Loved Ones please make these songs a part of your song collection. Request them on the radio and or dedicate them to someone or yourself. Buy them on Itunes.

QQ – Same Gun-this song will make you want to cry because you feel it to your heart for the youths of today.

Duane Stephenson – Truth Is

Duane Stephenson – Better Tomorrow

Duane Stephenson ft. Ras Shiloh – As Soon As We Rise

Morgan Heritage – Jealousy

Remember each song I give you has a meaning so listen to the lyrics and get the message.

I will not endorse any artist but will endorse the song because the songs represent something. If it did not I would not have been led there.

P.S.S. I am so not done because I forgot to tell all of you **TO HAVE A CONTINGENCY PLAN. A BACKUP PLAN.**

People not all plans are fool proof. Our ideas maybe great but you will have someone at the top to shoot you down. They will give you all the reasons for failure as well as stamp rejection on your application but do not give up. Always remember when one door close another one is opening. Some of us do not have the cash but start from home.

For example young man you want to make suck suck but your mother can't buy sugar. You have sugar cane in your back yard. Cut one, and mash it with a hammer or rock stone then squeeze the juice out of the cane. Let grandpa show you if you don't understand what I am saying and please health precautions. ***Keep everything clean and sanitary.***

What about colouring-flavour you are saying? Do you not have guava and passion fruit? Use them for flavour. Do you see where I am going with this? Use your head and be wise, think.

I am hearing I don't have bags. Well use an ice tray and stick tooth picks in the middle when the solution or your suck suck is almost set.

Where do you sell it?

Try at school, church on Sundays, or when your class mates are coming home from school.

Don't get discouraged if you don't make thousands of dollars in one day. If you make $100.00 that's one hundred dollars you did not have in your pocket. Do you understand? You are now doing something with yourself and remember you do have competition because you are going up against the bag and box juice market. I know you are small scale but hey every penny counts right.

What if the people don't want your product you are now saying as well as doubting yourself?

Market your product differently meaning you have all natural ingredients in your product, the box and bag juice have preservatives, artificial colouring yada yada yada. See where I am going with this? Which is better for your health? The product filled with preservatives or the all natural product?

To you Mr. Rich Man this also goes for you have a contingency plan if the original one does not work out.

For some of you that will be saying bamboo chairs is already being done and the market is flooded with makers do something different. Meaning and this is where I am going to be so wacked out because my brain sometimes work on a wacked out level.

How about messing bamboo with cotton to make a different and stronger type of material. You can call it the cotton bamboo. What about something synthetic if cotton cannot work or even silk. Weird I know but it could work. Jamaican's we can do anything we put our mind to. Run with this idea and see what you come up with. Come on UWI students what the hell are you going to school for. Put your practical knowledge and book knowledge to the test. Find the common ground for the two.

Some of you that are study chemistry and biochemistry I am going to throw this at you. It's wacked again but what about grass.

Whaaaaaaat?

What about grass? Jamaica has different types of grass and I am talking about the one-or the grass that cows all animals eat.

What nutritional content does it have for humans?

It's good for animals what about humans. Can we blend it to make tea?

Can it ward off or fight diseases?

Is it safe for human consumption?

Do you see where I am going with this?

If this grass or the grass that animals eat cannot work look into fever grass. We drink it for tea and animals eat it. What is it good for and when you find out start producing and introducing new organic products to the market. And people I know this will take years to develop and my ideas are crazy. But nothing tried nothing done meaning you have two choices. You can sit on your ass and laugh while another country run with these ideas and profit or you can get off your ass and do something.

Experiment with my ideas, see if they will work and help yourself in the process. If you choose to let my ideas go and another country say wait a minute that can work and it does work you Mr. Jamaican can't be jealous because I did come to you with these ideas and you shot it down calling me dumb and stupid even crazy.

Remember good ideas are always crazy to the world until someone comes along and take a chance and before you know it they have made a name for themselves.

All I am saying see if it will work. Maybe bamboo work well with something synthetic and not cotton. Hey I don't know all I have are ideas okay.

Don't stop thinking because sey mi chat bout the condominiums now a smart thinking person would say condo's buildings. Let me see if someone takes her up on the idea and start building condos maybe they won't come equipped with laundry mats. I can have a laundry mat.

The lights are going off now right?

How about a mini strip mall that houses a hair dressing salon, male and female clothing boutiques, and electronic store, a mini supermarket or a little ma and pa store, a food court or even a day care centre.

I am not into gambling but how about a government run casino. I know this is bad but I had to go there. Sorry people and God truly forgive me for suggesting it.

What about a store that sells only furniture. A furniture store.

Hey Mr. Government. Female Government I know but how about having another Ethanol plant in Jamaica and let people use it as an alternative mode of fuel instead of gasoline-oil. Think of the environment because Ethanol is cleaner than Gas. Do you even know the dangers to your health when you use gas? This could be government owned. Revenue would be coming in and if it is cheaper to produce why not. Just look into it.

Hey you can dub me the crazy lady okay. No don't dub me that. I truly love Jamaica that's all and if you hate me too bad. I will always love my country and the people. Well no I don't love the people. Naa I love the people because I get a friendly smile when I am there.

People for real go to the market Never change this cultural icon. Anyhow unnu stop di market or close them down mi an unnu. Oh yes people pay unnu taxes.

No for real you cannot have a business and not contribute to the upkeep of your country.

Mr. Government and people don't get mad at me now but what about business license for companies, corporations and shops. These ma and pa shops do they have a license. If they don't let them buy a business license and make these license expire every 5 years. Charge a renewal fee of $100.00 make this standard across the board for everyone and charge a license fee of

$500.00 to $10000.00 depending on the size of the business. All in Jamaican dollars of course no foreign currency.

Do the same for the churches as well. Charge them a license fee and a renewal fee. Use the same fee chart as above. No charge the churches a renewal fee of $74.00.

Like everyone else let them pay income tax. Each Pastor and Deacon must do income tax at the end of the year and if church employs people they have to pay the appropriate taxes for their services to the government.

For all of you that owe the government back taxes pay your taxes. Make some kind of arrangement to pay it. Come on you make the money. Shit tell wifey or hubby she can't have steak every night. Mi surely know sey shi can have chicken back sometimes. The money that you save on steaks can pay down some of your taxes. And no she can't have champagne every night shi too damn greedy and tell the mistress instead of getting $50000.00 each week she is only getting $25000.00 if shi complain lef har a road because sey shi naa think about you. Plus shi naa think about herself. Shi jus a think bout di greed and har pocket.

If you a pay fi har weekly and monthly bills cut back. Hey pum pum no rule. Well maybe it rules you but think. When the government clamp down on you where is she? Shi a dey pee pee cluck cluck behind you? I think not because all shi a go do is fine another Joe. I need not tell you about the blow.

That's it for now until I get another idea.

MICHELLE

Other books by Michelle Jean

Saving America for a woman's perspective

More Talk

Blackman Redemption

Love Bound

Love Bound book Two

Behind the Scars

Dedication Unto My Kids

Ode to Mr. Dean Fraser